PRACTICE
RESURRECTION

PRACTICE
RESURRECTION

and Other Essays

Erik Reece

COUNTERPOINT

Library of Congress Cataloging-in-Publication Data Is Available.

Cover design by Nick Gomez-Hall

ISBN: 978-1-64009-206-8

COUNTERPOINT
2560 Ninth Street, Suite 318
Berkeley, CA 94710
www.counterpointpress.com

Printed in the United States of America

For Wendell,
in memory of Guy

CONTENTS

help me
I am of the people the grass

blades touch

—George Oppen

PROLOGUE

....

SCENE: *The heads of Orpheus and John the Baptist are floating along a Mediterranean river.*

Conversation ensues.

> Q: What is the world?
> A: A self-creating God.
>
> Q: What is God?
> A: Being.
>
> Q: So you believe in God?
> A: I believe in the world as it exists.
>
> Q: That's what I meant.
> A: Wave!

NOTES FROM A VERY SMALL ISLAND

With my solo canoe loaded down by camping gear and a cooler full of beer, wine, and cold cuts, I paddle out onto Lake Umbagog, a beautiful eight-thousand-acre body of water that stretches across the Maine–New Hampshire border. Spear-shaped firs, spruces, and white cedars frame the lake in deep green hues. Otter, moose, and mink are said to prowl the marshy banks. I already see a solitary loon floating in the distance. The day is warm and bright, and a cool June breeze is combing narrow furrows onto the surface of the water. I balance the wind on the stem of my canoe with a paddle stroke my grandfather taught me thirty years ago. Back then we explored the coves and inlets near the Chesapeake Bay, where my grandparents lived in a small stucco parsonage. Some years later, my grandfather talked a fishing buddy of his into selling me this canoe for $100. My grandfather was a forceful country preacher, and people had a hard time telling him no. From the other room, I could overhear him saying into the phone, "Well Bill, he's just a poor graduate student."

By turning the paddle away from the stern at the end of the stroke, I carve the letter *J* into the water, a kind of one-letter poem that dissolves into a small eddy and must be reinscribed over and over. I remember, when I was a kid, watching from the bow seat of my grandfather's canoe as he performed the *J* stroke with a deft deliberateness. He handled his paddle with such a fluid ease, the water never even splashed around the blade as he turned it into the curve of the *J*. I try to emulate that artistry now. But once I reach the middle of Lake Umbagog, I find myself struggling against a strong headwind. After about two hours of paddling south, then east toward what I hope is the Maine border, I see the number 35 blazed in white on a boulder. I realize with a sudden thrill that this is my island. At least for the next several days, it is mine alone.

The bow of my canoe eases to a halt between two exposed roots of a tall cedar that stands on the sandy shore. The island is about the size of a football field. It is all wooded except for a small clearing, where a picnic table sits next to a stone fire pit. I haul my gear out and pitch my tent on a bed of pine needles. I set my portable kitchen (which amounts to a propane stove, a burnt pot, and a fork) on the picnic table and unroll my sleeping bag inside my small tent. Thus ensconced, I pour some white wine into my blue metal camp cup and take a stroll around the grounds. A small archipelago of stones and boulders defines the northern tip of the island, while at the southern end, I find one wild orchid, a pink lady slipper, growing in the shade of pine trees. Its single seed must have blown over from the mainland a few hundred feet away. The flower, which looks like a pale, slightly deflated wind sock, is the only thing blooming on the island.

The island straddles the state line, so that walking west to east, about forty yards from shore to shore, I cross over from New Hampshire into Maine. A bifurcated white birch stands in the middle of the island near my campsite, and I amuse myself by imagining that the state line cuts right between its forked truck. What taxes might I incur simply by walking from one side of the island to the next? Had I an automobile on Island 35 (a ridiculous thought), I'd have to buckle up as I crossed over into Maine. New Hampshire remains the only state in the Union with no seat belt law. Consequently, some have proposed that the state motto, "Live free or die," be changed to "Live free *and* die." I sympathize, though, with the anticonstraint crowd. As one who refuses to wear a seat belt on (admittedly shaky) libertarian grounds, I raise my cup to the independent spirit of the Granite State.

Because I live in Kentucky, I am surprised at how early the sun rises in these northern latitudes. I find myself up at six, making coffee on my island still shrouded in mist. I toss out the dregs of last night's wine and replace them with traditionally terrible camp coffee. Sugar improves it though, and as I sit in my folding chair, the cool air and the hot coffee cast a promising feel over the day. Out in the lake, fish are rising up to snatch midges and mayflies from the surface of the water. Slowly the sun starts to burn the mist off the lake.

On a small island—particularly *alone* on a small island—one has the sense of standing outside all institutions. Here, the only rule I must follow is: take only notes; leave only feces. For the latter, there is a discreetly placed privy in the middle of the island, surrounded by shrubs. The island is also our most persistent metaphor for solitude. And solitude, we are told, is the condition out of which philosophy arises. I myself have no ambitions for making any contribution to the field this week, but I have brought with me a slim volume of the pre-Socratic philosopher Heraclitus (translated by classicist-modernist Guy Davenport). Actually, a volume of Heraclitus, by definition, must be slim, since all that has come down to us are fragments—epigrams on philosophy, nature, and the human mind. And because a canoe, unlike a backpack, lends itself to transporting a small library, I have also brought along a few books by other men who lived alone and in their aloneness contemplated the fragments of Heraclitus: Friedrich Nietzsche, Thomas Merton, Guy Davenport. Nietzsche called Heraclitus "the royally secluded, all-sufficing Heraclitus." Between 540 and 480 BCE, the Greek philosopher wrote from an island of his own choosing, a self-imposed exile outside the city of Ephesos. Like Nietzsche, Heraclitus was considered by his contemporaries elitist and reclusive. And like an itinerate street preacher named Yeshua, Heraclitus spoke in images that suggest meaning but do not spell it out. Much remains left to the reader.

Every collection of his fragments begin with this passage:

> The Logos is eternal
> but men have not heard it
> or men have heard it and not understood.

> Through the Logos all things are understood
> yet men do not understand
> as you shall see when you put acts and words to the test I am
>   going to propose:

> One must talk about everything according to its nature,
>   how it comes to be and how it grows.
> Men have talked about the world without paying attention to
>   the world or to their own minds,
> as if they were asleep or absent-minded.

For Heraclitus, the Logos was not the "word made flesh," as in the Gospel of John, but rather, in Martin Heidegger's translation, "the primal gathering principle" of the natural world. It is the invisible syntax that holds individual beings together, and because it is invisible, it can only be known intuitively. Fundamentally, we might think of the Logos as an ecological principle that affirms the natural world's interdependence. It marries the hawk moth to the primrose, the lichen's fungi to its algae. Each element of the natural world follows the law of its own nature, an internal Logos, which is also reflected in the higher principle that gathers all things together. Thus Emerson would write, "Within man is the soul of the whole." The problem with man, observed Heraclitus, is that he doesn't hold true to *his* own nature. He talks about the world and his own mind without actually paying attention to either.

Heraclitus wrote in the third fragment, "Men who wish to know about the world must learn about it in its particular details." We must leave the realm of abstract law, particularly the realm of the *ought,* and return to the realm of science and poetry—the place of particulars. The American poet A. R. Ammons, who wrote with a very clear-eyed attention to the natural world, once said in an interview, "I have tried [in my poetry] to get rid of the Western tradition as much as possible. . . . I really do want to begin with a bare space with streams and rocks and trees." Then he added, in reference to Heraclitus, "If I get back to the pre-Socratics, I feel that I'm in the kind of world that I would enjoy to be in." The Western tradition, after Heraclitus, too often disparaged the natural world as *only* appearance, only a shadow on a cave wall. For these thinkers, the truth lay somewhere else and could be understood only by men who turned from the world toward either the ascetic purity of the Christian tradition or the abstract philosophy of the Platonic tradition. Heraclitus, like the Buddhists of China and Japan, simply accepted the natural world as he found it. It was neither good nor bad. Heraclitus believed we must look at the world as the First Parents did *before* they ate from the Tree of the Knowledge of Good and Evil. He was not only a pre-Socratic thinker; he was a prelapsarian thinker. The world needs no justification. It simply *is.* Sitting in my canvas chair, staring out at the calm blue lake, I feel this twenty-five-hundred-year-old observation to be profoundly contemporary. More to the point, I feel it to be profoundly *necessary*.

After a breakfast of instant grits and Vermont sausage, I paddle from island to island, looking for other wild orchids, hoping maybe to see a moose along the shore. Clouds cast blue shadows into the pockets of the green ridge sides that surround the lake. Now and then, the wind sweeps up a small chop on the open water and my canoe cuts across the blue waves with a cleaving rock of the bow. Then everything settles down again. The loons issue their seemingly random calls from the middle of the lake. A couple of mergansers lower their landing gear and settle down on the water not far from my canoe. We all just float.

There is a quiet intensity to a day like this. It almost makes you shaky. I lie flat in my canoe, with my head on my life jacket, and close my eyes. I imagine myself as a seed inside its pod, a violin lying quiet in its case. Thoreau wrote that when floating on Walden Pond, he sometimes stopped existing and began to be. I think it is a crucial transition, that move from merely existing into an experience of clarity and presence that truly deserves to be called *being*. Here I can read the wind and the water from the bow seat of my canoe. While I experience and observe Heraclitus's tenet that only change is unchanging, I sometimes feel as if I inhabit a moment with neither a past nor a future. Paddling back to my island around dusk, I notice whirligig beetles that look like little black seeds, spinning across the surface of the water near my canoe. According to my field guide, each one's eyes have two parts, with which it can see above and below the surface of the water at the same time. It is as if these water striders inhabit two worlds. "Eyes are better informers than ears," wrote Heraclitus. As I grew into adulthood, I often felt I would have been better served as a child if I had spent more time in my grandfather's canoe, observing the ducks and ospreys in the marshy coves around his parsonage, and less time sitting in his church, listening to dire sermons about my woeful inadequacies before God. My grandfather was really two different men inside the unroofed church of his canoe and inside the whitewashed walls of his sanctuary. And since his death, I have struggled to reconcile the master paddler, the man who loved the mountains and rivers of Virginia, with the man who preached that we live in a fallen world from which we are in desperate need of salvation.

About fifteen years ago, shortly after he retired from the ministry, my grandfather admitted to me something I never thought I'd hear him say—he might have been wrong. "Sometimes I wake up in the middle of the night," he confessed, "stricken with the fear that, all these years, I might have been preaching the wrong thing." Specifically, he might have been wrong to preach such a punishing message of guilt, sin, and blood sacrifice. Perhaps he had been too hard on his congregation. Perhaps he had emphasized the apostle Paul's gospel of fear at the expense of Jesus's teaching of love and forgiveness. This admission both shocked and relieved me. Finally, I thought, my grandfather and I might talk honestly about religion and the inevitable doubts that accompany one's faith. I had my share of doubts, compounded by a secret sense of guilt that I had betrayed my grandfather's religion, and so betrayed my grandfather. And for a while we did have interesting conversations about whether Paul had really understood Jesus's message or whether he had distorted it into something Jesus himself would not have recognized.

But gradually, as my grandfather's health failed, as his relationship with my only uncle deteriorated into a tense, ugly silence, and as my grandmother drifted slowly into a quiet dementia, I watched my grandfather return to his earlier belief that this world is a realm of disappointments, a toilsome proving ground where we strive to earn admittance into heaven. Late in life, he would bring himself to tears at the dinner table when, during a rambling blessing of the food, he began contemplating the pain Jesus must have suffered to save him, my grandfather, from this sinful world. By then I had come to believe, as it says in the Gospel of Luke, that "the kingdom of God is before us," spread gloriously across the natural world; but my grandfather had wholly abandoned that idea and was hoping desperately for a kingdom on high, something better than the mortal pain of this earthly realm.

Thirty years earlier, his son, my father, had committed suicide. He had followed his own father into the ministry but never seemed comfortable at his own pulpit, and he lacked my grandfather's fist-pounding conviction. My uncle, my father's only brother, made three suicide attempts of his own before descending into a pharmacological torpor and eventually organ failure. For years, I had wanted my grandfather to accept some responsibility for both of his sons' despair. More specifically, I wanted him to acknowledge that the church, and his own punishing version of Christianity, bore some of the blame.

Heraclitus thought that too often we let other people tell us what our own minds are like. I think this was my father's fatal mistake And it is one I inherited. I let my grandfather, whom I loved profoundly, tell me what my mind should be like, how pure my thoughts should be, until I felt as if my life had become, under his stern tutelage, one great act of renunciation. Everything worldly—the sensuous, the intoxicating, the aesthetically pleasing—was suspect, a temptation. Nietzsche, himself the son of a minister, wrote that in Christianity, "I never fail to see a *hostility to life*." In my grandfather's church, this hostility was strong indeed. With my grandmother at the organ, the congregation would sing, "This world is not my home." It is a sentiment that infuses much of American fundamentalism and much of mainstream Christianity. But it is one I came gradually to distrust, until I finally decided that if I was going to escape my father's fate, I would have to abandon my grandfather's beliefs altogether.

However, unlike the "conversion experience" to Christianity, disbe-lief is not a cataclysmic event. In my experience, I found that reli-gious convictions vanish more like mist off the water. You can't say when they disappeared, but you know they are gone for good. Then, what you have left is the world, its mountains and rivers and lakes, which you tell yourself are the lineaments, and the blood flowing through the veins, of a more enduring god.

At dusk, I watch through binoculars as a beaver noses across the water toward its lodge near the shore, patrolled by a group of grackle and sandpipers. The mosquitoes and horseflies were quite bad on my first night in camp (much larger than their southern cousins), so I attempt to combat them with fire on night two. Scouring the island for fallen limbs and driftwood, I find, in the dry brush on the north end, a foot-long piece of a birch branch, one inch in diameter. Its bark is smooth and deep reddish brown. A beaver has sharpened one end to almost pencil-like precision. It occurs to me that if my island were suddenly besieged by, I don't know, say hostile seat belt enthusiasts, this sharpened birch branch might help stave off an attack. I decide to keep it in my tent, next to my sleeping bag. I also find a piece of driftwood that looks as if it has been deliberately sculpted into something that would not seem out of place in a modern art museum. It has a kind of base, and as I set it on the picnic table, it evokes something vaguely fig-urative, some prehistoric creature of the sea. Yet it has also been smoothed by water into an abstraction that the modern sculptor Constantin Brancusi would have admired. A series of intricate, wavelike patterns weaves across the dry gray bark, as if for years Lake Umbagog has been writing its own autobiography on this soft, impressionable wood. Its artistry seems to be of the purist form. The piece of wood has been shaped by the most elemental forces—wind and water, perhaps even fire—the same forces that

Brancusi strove to emulate in his own work. Guy Davenport has written, "What is most modern in our time frequently turns out to be the most archaic." One might add that this little piece of drift-wood was fashioned by the most archaic forces of all. Davenport further observed that our modern passion for the archaic in art "is a longing for something lost, for energies, values, and certainties unwisely abandoned by an industrial age." This seems absolutely correct to me. I suppose it is the same longing that caused me to heave my canoe into the back of my truck and drive halfway across the country to this lake, with its preindustrial solitude. Perhaps I came here to enact some urge buried deep in my genetic past, and thus deep inside myself. A primitive boat and a primitive paddle brought me to a campsite, described as "primitive" on my map of Lake Umbagog. And here I feel I am at the source of something. The source of the Androscoggin River, in fact, but also the source of some unmediated, authentic experience.

I crumple up the local paper I bought in town, build a teepee of kindling, then stack some fallen branches around the kindling. The wood is dry and a fire catches quickly. The mosquitoes seem only partially deterred by my blazing pyre, so I pull on a long-sleeve shirt and settle in for an evening of fire-gazing. "Everything is made of fire," claimed Heraclitus. What is fascinating about this ancient remark is how it turned out to be so improbably true. Werner Heisenberg, one of the twentieth century's most important nuclear physicists, wrote in *Physics and Philosophy* that "modern physics is in some way extremely near to the doctrines of Heraclitus." He went on, "If we replace the word 'fire' by the word 'energy' we can almost repeat his statements word for word from the modern point of view." Heisenberg also approved of the way Heraclitus resolved the persistent nagging philosophical problem of the *one and the many*—if the world is made up of so many different forms, can there be any one thing that *unifies* them?—by positing that the world comes into being through a positive form of strife. "Opposites cooperate," wrote Heraclitus. Heisenberg contended that since the theory of relativity states that mass and energy are the same concepts, "The strife between opposites in the philosophy of Heraclitus can be found in the strife between two different forms of energy." Twenty-five hundred years later, Heisenberg found the thinking of Heraclitus much closer to modern physics than that of any philosopher who followed him.

Furthermore, not only did Heraclitus continue to study the natural world through its particulars, he did not try to separate himself from it as philosophy had done from Socrates up to Descartes. It was Descartes, most profoundly, whose philosophy created a terrible sense of separateness between mind and body, human beings and the natural world. He destroyed the Logos, the gathering principle, by reducing the world to a set of *objects* that had little connection to one another.

In important ways, quantum physics rescues us from the tyranny of Descartes and returns us to the Heraclitean point of view. In the late 1920s, Heisenberg and Niels Bohr discovered that they could not observe the goings-on of the subatomic world without altering what they saw by the very act of observing it. Thus both the science of Heisenberg and the philosophy of Heraclitus undermined the traditional Cartesian belief that man can stand outside nature, against nature, and moreover that man can manipulate and destroy nature without suffering the fate of a species that is itself an interdependent part of that world. The object is really only another subject.

But if Heisenberg understood the Heraclitean fire as an analog to subatomic physics, the Trappist monk Thomas Merton saw it as a religious force, an inner light that fuses our connection to the Logos. Merton lived for three decades at the Gethsemane Monastery near Bardstown, Kentucky, a town known more for its bourbon than its piety. For many years, Merton resided alone in a hermitage at the edge of the monastery, where he contemplated pine trees and wrote some of the twentieth century's most beautiful meditations on man and God. He interpreted Heraclitus as saying, "Our spiritual and mystical destiny is to 'awaken' to the fire that is within us, and our happiness depends on the harmony in conflict that results from this awakening. Our vocation is a call to spiritual oneness in and with the logos." Merton seemed to agree with Heisenberg that a fire—the Logos—does indeed pervade all things and holds all things together. Whether this is a subatomic principle or a religious belief in a divine presence that suffuses all of nature doesn't really matter. Heraclitus was writing before philosophy had become a discipline. In the pre-Socratic world, thinking had not been divided into religion, science, poetry, or psychology. Perhaps this is why Heidegger felt so strongly that when philosophy moved indoors, when it became a "study of the schools," it abandoned *being* by dividing thinking from the Logos; it turned the Logos into an unnatural logic that falsely convinced *Homo sapiens* he was a rational animal, and therefore above the laws of nature. After Heraclitus, philosophy turned away from the practical and aesthetic question "How do we accomplish being in this world?" to the metaphysical question "What is truth?"

I think about the coniferous woods that surround Lake Umbagog, now cast in silhouette against the darkening sky. In each tree, in each species, there resides an innate intelligence that says, "We have found our niche; we have figured out the answer to your first question." As for the second question, the trees reply, "It never occurred to us to ask." Paddling around on Lake Umbagog, it never occurs to me either. But I think of how this question of truth—the Ultimate Truth—obsessed my grandfather to the point that he made it nearly impossible for his sons to try to find an answer to the first question, one that would have allowed them to find some accommodation, maybe even some happiness, in this world.

And it wasn't just my grandfather. It seems to me that a great majority of us human animals have become so consumed with the second, ultimately unanswerable question that we have done a very poor job of accomplishing being, and of allowing others to be— namely the 8.7 million or so other species with whom we share the planet. *Homo sapiens* is in the middle of creating the earth's sixth mass extinction, due largely to overpopulation, overconsumption, pollution, and the destruction of other species' habitat. Climate change alone could destroy 25 percent of all plants and animals on the planet by 2050 and 50 percent by the end of the century. It is by no means an exaggeration to say that the monotheistic nations, those obsessed with their own *one truth*, are largely responsible for bringing the world to this brink. Indigenous cultures and Eastern religions have traditionally been far more concerned with the question of *being* over the question of *truth*. As Nietzsche put it, "Buddhism does not promise but fulfills; Christianity promises everything but fulfills nothing." That is, Buddhism "fulfills" by placing the kingdom of God before us, in the here and now. And really, herein lies our greatest modern sin: we do not love the world enough.

Each night, something spooks the loons and I awake to hear a crazed tremolo that sends a shiver through the darkness. In the morning, two tree swallows are courting in the branches of a maple that hangs over the water. The male darts in small, mischievous circles around his mate, picking at her tail feathers. The last time I came to this lake, I was married. Happily, I thought at the time, or at least happily enough. But slowly, my wife and I turned into strangers. Nietzsche said (though it's odd that he would have known) that a marriage should be a long conversation. Our conversation slowly, quite literally drifted into an awkward silence. Then one day I walked out of that life and into this one. I bought a small house with a big enough yard for a nice vegetable garden and a chicken coop. It's in an old neighborhood with wide front porches and a corner store. I can walk there for groceries, as well as to the university where I teach and to the downtown movie theater that shows independent films. My life has taken on a somewhat Heraclitean feel. I find myself single, childless, unbeholden. And I find myself thinking of two other unbeholden, Heraclitean walkers: Thoreau and Nietzsche. Nietzsche said that walking *was* thinking, and he spent hours doing both in the mountains surrounding Turin, Italy. Thoreau declared himself a saunterer by occupation and even invented an etymology for the word: *sans terre,* meaning to be without land, and therefore at home wherever he went. Thoreau would spend six hours a day walking the forests and fields of Concord. And out of such solitude came *Walden,* just as out of Nietzsche's mountain rambles came his masterpiece, *Thus Spoke Zarathustra.*

Did they need their solitude to incubate their genius? Would marriage and family life have redirected their energies, softened their uncompromising critiques of Western bourgeois civilization? It is obviously quite possible to write great books surrounded by family; Dickens and George Sand managed it quite well. But I think there are certain books—*Walden* and *Zarathustra,* for instance—that can only come out of a deep solitude, perhaps even a *wounded* solitude. After they had each been rebuffed in their proposals of marriage, Nietzsche turned to the Alps and Thoreau turned to the rivers and ponds of Concord. In the wilderness, they each practiced and articulated the art of *self-invention.* They replaced the Socratic call to *know oneself* with the Heraclitean injunction to *become who you are.*

Can such a philosophy of self-invention still be accomplished within a marriage, within a family, within a community? For the sake of our survival as social animals, we had better hope so. But the solitary experiments of Nietzsche and Thoreau, because they are solitary, throw the act of self-invention into dramatic relief.

Everything else is cleared from the stage so that we can watch the natural philosopher, in Thoreau's case, strip his life to the bare essentials, so he can then build it back up according to his own needs and his own nature. Nietzsche's invocation of a new man, a free spirit, an "immoralist," was not, as has often been said, a sign of his nihilistic elitism; it was rather a call for Germans, for Americans, for modern men and women, to become much more *interesting* people. The great enemy in Nietzsche's writing, as in Heraclitus's, is *mediocrity*. Nietzsche vied against modern Christianity precisely because it encouraged a herd mentality, a loss of originality, an unthinking acceptance of a moral code that seemed to him too hostile to life. Morality should *affirm* life (Nietzsche loved italics) in all of its manifestations, not deny it. To invent a self, a morality, a *style*—that, for Nietzsche, meant to elevate one's life to the level of a work of art.

Being: it's a big subject. Too big, alas, for the language we've invented to discuss and define it. But too often, I think, we have tended to use language as a cage, something that traps words inside rigid definitions. And because, as a species, we have never been able to agree on those definitions, and because language has never been able to objectively represent the world around us, some of the most important modern philosophers—Nietzsche, Heidegger, Ludwig Wittgenstein, and Richard Rorty—have called for an "end of philosophy." More specifically, they have called for a turn, or a return, to literature and poetry. Looking back on his first book, *The Birth of Tragedy*, Nietzsche wrote in 1886, "What I had to say then—too bad that I did not dare say it as a poet: perhaps I had the ability." And after one of Rorty's lectures, and right after John Rawls's book *A Theory of Justice* was published, I heard Rorty tell a student, "I don't want to define justice; I just want to tell stories." Which is another way of saying, let's abandon the question of truth for the question of accomplishing being. Through the subjective stories of the tribe, we learn to find accommodation in the landscapes we inhabit. In an essay called "Symbolism: Communication or Communion?" Thomas Merton made the helpful observation that while science and philosophy aim at communication through signs, the highest form of poetry achieves a level of communion. "Symbolism," he writes, "strives to 'bring together' man, nature, and God in a living and sacred synthesis." All three—man the poet, God the animating breath, nature the image—converge there, in the symbol. If the scientific sign classifies the things of the world, the poetic symbol reconciles them, and us with them. It bridges the split between subject and object, as if to replace the divisive *logic* of the Tree of Knowledge with an earlier poetry of the Logos. As Merton wrote over and over in his late work, to unify subject and object means to once again achieve the sense of being that Thoreau described when floating on Walden Pond.

Art is a better interpreter of life than morality is. That's the conclusion Nietzsche reached in *The Birth of Tragedy*. The early Greeks, the founders of tragedy, did not try to explain away life's suffering as something they deserved because they had disobeyed God (indeed, there was nothing at all moral about their gods). But that is not to say the Greeks didn't suffer. Rather they transformed suffering, gave it shape, through art. Then, by inventing the Olympian world, and by telling the story of gods and men through tragedy, they created a kind of trinity out of art, religion, and the natural world.

Like Thoreau, Nietzsche preferred the Greek gods to the Judeo-Christian God because the Greek deities did not judge the world but rather *justified* it as what Nietzsche called "an aesthetic phenomenon," a work of art. They did not stand apart from the world but rather, as Yahweh did in the prelapsarian world, they strolled through the garden in the cool of the evening. To raise one's experiences to the level of art is to make them worthy of contemplation. Then life takes on the same qualities as art: it gains intensity,

vividness, resonance, meaning. And by Nietzsche's logic, to trans-
form one's life into a work of art would be to achieve the divine
in this world. The natural world would then indeed appear as the
kingdom of God. But this aesthetic impulse, so strong in Nietzsche,
was not enough to justify my own father's life to himself. And what I
keep coming back to is this: the unbearable Christian belief that he
had inherited the congenital sinfulness of Adam; that he was born
broken, into a terrible separateness, blinded my father to seeing this
world as anything other than a life best left behind.

The Logos of John's Gospel is God made flesh in order to redeem
human beings, through blood sacrifice, *from* this world. The Logos
of Heraclitus is just the opposite. It is the great Intuition that redeems *this* world *as it is.* Nietzsche, Heidegger, Thoreau—these are
the true heirs of Heraclitus because after "the end of philosophy,"
they urge us to return to the earlier question of how do we find
meaning—how we *make* meaning—in *this* world. And at the end of
philosophy, the way we both find and make it is through the language of belonging.

Poetry, I think, is the ultimate language of belonging, of accommodation. Recall that before the First Parents ate from the Tree of
the Knowledge of Good and Evil, before they became moralists,
they were, in essence, poets. They did not judge the world; they
simply affirmed it. When Yahweh marched all the animals of the
garden before Adam and asked what he—*Homo loquax*—wanted to
name them, Adam created the names out of the same substance—
the *pneuma,* breath—with which Yahweh had called the world into
being (and because the Greek *pneuma* can be translated as both
"breath" and "spirit," we can say that it was out of *inspiration* that
Adam named the animals). Yahweh did not intend the natural
world to be a courtroom where sin is measured along a continuum
of good and evil; he intended it to be a work of art. And like all
great works of art, it was a realm governed by its own internal laws:

improvisation, adaptation, complementarity, and harmonic tensions. The talking animals were meant to follow these natural laws. They were meant, as Heraclitus said, to be "an organic continuation of the Logos." They were not meant to sever that connection and, as a consequence, become judges, priests, or literary critics. They were certainly not meant, like the six characters in Pirandello's famous play, to go in search of their author. What characters do that? The notion is as absurd as Pirandello meant it to be. No, the talking animals were meant—we were meant—to be caretakers, both through language and in actions. "Man is not the lord of beings," wrote Heidegger. "Man is the shepherd of Being."

Poetry, I think, is the ultimate language of belonging. Unlike Plato's realm of eternal forms or the apostle Paul's eternal salvation, the best poetry calls us back to *this world*. To overcome all the painful acts of separation that followed man's expulsion from the Garden— that is the work of poetry. Poetry calls us back to it, but this time with a greater sense of meaning, a greater sense of belonging. The true poem captures not just what is seen but the *experience of seeing*. Poetry, we might say, is the aura thrown around an ordinary object to show that, in fact, it isn't ordinary at all. The poem then is a microcosm, held together by its own invisible Logos, that shows us how to transcend the mistake of seeing the world as merely a collection of objects, separate and insignificant. Poetry is a religion that redeems us *back* into this world. It couldn't save my father, but I think it might save me.

Sitting on the rock emblazoned with the number 35, I watch a solitary loon through a pair of binoculars. The plumage on its wings is black and white and looks from here like a complicated musical score. Its head is dark black and its eyes bright red. The loon floats, preens, dives, bears its white breast skyward.

The floating life. I've been practicing it for the last few days—paddling, writing, watching—and I am beginning (again) to understand its many virtues. Every now and then, the loon lets out a short yodel or dives for a fish. Since it sits, or floats, at the top of the food chain, the adult loon has no predators; it can afford these idle days.

Still, this apparent nonchalance is deceptive. Northern loons are now dying at an accelerated, unnatural rate. And the reason has a lot to do with where I come from. In the eastern part of my home state, Kentucky, strip miners are blasting off the tops of mountains so they can harvest, as quickly as possible, the thin seams of coal that lie hundreds of feet below. Everything that isn't coal is bulldozed down into the valleys below. The water is toxic, floods are constant, and much of the air isn't fit to breathe. After these Appalachian mountains are destroyed, their coal is trucked off to fire the power plants that provide half of the United States' electricity. When that coal is burned, it releases into the air not only the greenhouse gas carbon dioxide but also mercury—forty-eight tons of it each year. Wind currents carry the mercury hundreds of miles to the northeast, where it works its way up the food chain from plankton to crayfish to fish, then to the loons. That mercury severely damages the loons' central nervous system, harms vision, and is extremely toxic to developing embryos. One-fifth of the loons tested by US Fish and Wildlife are contaminated with enough mercury to disrupt breeding.

And it isn't just the loons that are sick. They, like their emblematic predecessor, the canary in the coal mine, are a sign of human problems as well. After all, it isn't only loons that eat fish. A National Academy of Sciences report warns that sixty thousand babies born each year in the United States could be exposed to enough mercury in utero to cause permanent brain damage. And during the first decade of the 2000s, the Bush administration consistently worked to weaken regulations on the release of mercury into air and water.

"The mind of man exists in a logical universe but is not itself logical," wrote Heraclitus in a key fragment. Why else would we knowingly contaminate the air we breathe and the food we eat? Why would we risk our children's health just so we can air-condition houses that are on average 50 percent bigger than they were thirty years ago? Why else would we—I'm speaking of Americans now, who make up only 5 percent of the world's population—generate 25 percent of the carbon dioxide that is causing our global climate crisis?

One can examine any healthy watershed to see that the natural world is itself "logical," governed by the Logos. A forest demonstrates an intelligence it has been honing for millions of years. From the level of the canopy, down through the understory to the shrub layer, the herb and fern layer, and finally the soil layer of decomposing leaves, forests form intensely symbiotic communities. Bees pollinate wildflowers; leaf shredders serve up food at the headwaters of streams; termites break down dead logs; worms aerate soil around plant roots; squirrels distribute acorns. Each species finds its niche and learns to adapt, through cooperation, to its surroundings. Each species depends on another and so has a stake in maintaining the health of the entire forest community, the entire watershed. In the broadleaf forests closest to where I live, the mixed mesophytic, seventy different species of trees have learned to coexist interdependently, sharing light and resources. Hemlocks and beech keep to the streams, oak and hickories share the middle elevations, and pines form the high, dry crowns of the ridgetops. The flora and fauna have worked out a complex charter whereby each species inhabits its own niche. There is no waste, no imbalance, no "progress."

But man, said Heraclitus, "who is an organic continuation of the Logos, thinks he can sever that continuity and exist apart from it." If traces of three hundred industrial chemicals can be found in the umbilical cords of American newborns, if we have brought on a cataclysmic change in the climate, if we are destroying habitat at a rate by which we will lose 50 percent of all species by the next century, and if we are consuming natural resources so rapaciously that little will be left for our grandchildren, by what definition is this progress? By what definition is this "logical"? That is to say, why, when, how did we, the clever animal, adopt the supremely illogical notion that we can have infinite economic growth on a planet of finite resources? I believe that the fundamental reason we have adopted such an unsustainable, unhealthy, and unsympathetic way of thinking is because, as Heraclitus said, we have severed our connection to the Logos. We have let the logic of the strip mine replace the Logos of the forest.

The Greek word *ethos* translates into English as "dwelling place." To find the holy here, to find the kingdom of God before us—that could be the beginning of a new ethos, a new way of dwelling in the natural world. The great naturalist Aldo Leopold called this way of thinking—and acting—*the land ethic*. It means that we, the talking animals, must stop thinking of ourselves as conquerors of the land and must start understanding our roles as members of a land community. Anyone who has ever seen a mountain blown apart knows what conquerors of the land can do, what they are capable of. I don't think we yet know what members of a land community might accomplish. But to begin, we must, as Leopold famously said, start thinking like the mountain. We cannot simply think about the deer, or the trees, or the coal. We must listen to the Logos; we must start thinking again about the wholeness of being.

On my fifth morning on the island, I wake to find the sky darkening and my cooler empty. I hastily stuff my gear into a large, waterproof pack and break camp. As I paddle away, I am accompanied by that complex emotion many travelers experience—the draw of home, coupled with regret at having to leave this lake and this island. In the distance, I can see the blue speck that is my truck. Soon it will be taking me back to those patterns and routines known as real life. For the last few days, I have lived suspended in a prelapsarian fantasy, in a realm at once real and imagined. Obviously, the Heraclitean ethos of dwelling rightly must be applied to how one dwells among others as well as how one dwells alone on an island in the middle of a lake. Solidarity must be the sequel to solitude. To practice daily the art of belonging to this world—to belong to it wholly and sparingly, with humility and sympathy—that would be the truly heroic accomplishment. When I have my canoe packed back onto my truck and I drive back south, I will have time to think about these things. But for now, my paddle takes the measure of the moment and does not find it lacking.

STYLIST NEEDED:
REMEMBERING GUY DAVENPORT

G uy Davenport died on a gray winter morning in January 2005. As if on cue, my watch stopped working that day, which made me think of W. H. Auden's elegy for William Butler Yeats, who also, as it turned out, died in January. But Auden doesn't say that the clocks stopped, as I wrongly remembered, but rather,

> The mercury sank in the mouth of the dying day.
> O all the instruments agree
> The day of his death was a dark cold day.

On that dark cold day more than ten years ago, I stood on my front porch with Guy's companion of thirty years, Bonnie Jean Cox. We exchanged the usual and inadequate words that follow death. Then Bonnie turned to me and said, "I think only a few of us truly understood the innocence of Guy's mind."

The earth did not, as Auden said of Yeats, receive an honored guest. Guy's corpse, ravaged by a lifetime of chronic smoking, was left to the University of Kentucky's Markey Cancer Center for research. On an early spring day later that year, about fifty of us—his family members, former students, friends, and colleagues—gathered at the University of Kentucky's arboretum and memorialized Guy with a simple plaque set beneath a handsome sweet gum tree. The plaque read: EVERY FORCE EVOLVES A FORM. Bonnie Jean chose the inscription from one of Guy's titles, itself a statement by Shaker founder Mother Ann Lee. Guy, it could be said, admired equally the modernist architecture of Le Corbusier and the Shaker broom. ("It is a broom that means business," he once wrote.) A coherent culture, like the nineteenth-century Shaker village not far from where Guy lived in Lexington, Kentucky, is full of forces that make themselves intelligent through art, architecture, and artisanship.

The force that was Guy Davenport evolved and evoked a protean arsenal of forms: poems, stories, essays, novels, translations, paintings, wooden tables, even a fried bologna sandwich that he would serve up for dinner, assuming you would eat it. I ate many of them. Sometimes we would stand in the old-fashioned kitchen of his house at 621 Sayre Avenue and eat the sandwiches right over the frying pan. A large poster of the moon hung on the opposite wall. It was a satellite that fascinated Guy—the lonely, distant moon. We might gaze at it for a moment and then Guy would turn and say, "Want a Snickers?"

Several years before Guy's death, before we knew how bad the lung cancer had become, his publisher, Jack Shoemaker, asked him to send a recent photo for the spring catalog of Counterpoint Press. Since I had a new digital camera, Guy asked me to take the picture. I walked him down the street to a beauty salon. Out in front stood a yard sign that read simply:

STYLIST
NEEDED

I sat Guy down beside the sign and took the picture. I don't think Jack Shoemaker ever used it in his press material, but the photo amused Guy and he sent copies of it to correspondents. And that's what Guy was more than anything—a stylist. In an age of minimalists, Guy was a maximalist. His writing was a high wire act in every sense. The sound, the balance, the color of a sentence mattered. Guy was, I have come to believe, the greatest prose stylist of his generation. Cynthia Ozick comes close, Don DeLillo comes close, but sentence for sentence, no one can match Guy for the sheer elegance and virtuosity of his prose. If that were it, that would be enough. But Guy was also one of the most inventive writers of his generation. To my thinking, only Donald Barthelme was more audacious, more daring. When the American Academy and Institute of Arts and Letters bestowed upon Guy the Morton Dauwen Zabel Award for fiction, Donald Barthelme shook his hand at the ceremony and said, "I read you in hardback." It is a wonderfully oblique compliment from one master artificer to another.

What would have naturally been the dining room of the house Guy turned into his office. In the center of it sat a large table he had made himself, modeled after one Ezra Pound built in the twenties for his Paris apartment. The De Stijl–inspired table was the size of a front door, and in the center sat Guy's large electric typewriter. Guy kept up a voluminous correspondence, and he would reply to *everyone* who wrote him, however cracked or misguided the correspondent seemed. For hours each afternoon, Guy sat at his table and composed beautiful, high-spirited letters. I can conjure the image easily in my mind. Light is slanting through old blinds that hang in the front windows, falling across the potted plant on one corner of the table and books stacked around the typewriter. To Guy's left, a small metal stand holds up the letter to which he is responding, and to his right, smoke curls up from the ever-present cigarette resting in a black ashtray. On a well-worn oriental rug, a gray cat drowses in the sun. The news is on the radio. Guy listens for a moment, then looks at the cat and says, "Did you hear that Felix? George Bush just started another fucking war."

At that same table, Guy also transposed and transformed passages from his journals into the experiments—he preferred the word *assemblages*—that became his stories. Guy alternately bemoaned and bragged that he had only thirteen readers. Though he received hundreds of letters of fan mail, each new fan was inducted into that cabal of thirteen who had somehow found his message in a bottle. Guy waved off the accusation that his art was elitist. "Calling art elitist is like calling money valuable," he countered. That is to say, art is by nature elitist because so few can actually pull it off. Still, he admired many artists, such as Eudora Welty, who one would not call elitist. And he loved the British working-class films of Mike Leigh. Though he had no TV, Guy watched videos and DVDs with Bonnie Jean, at her house, six blocks from his. The greatest compliment I ever heard Guy pay another artist was when he said, "When Mike Leigh gets to heaven, Chekhov will want to shake his hand."

Guy once wrote, "Art is the attention we pay to the wholeness of the world." I think that single sentence defines his philosophy, his *art poetica*, his reason for sitting down at the typewriter or the easel every day. The purpose of art is to remind us *to pay attention* to the wholeness of the world or to what Guy also liked to call "the wholeness of being." That wholeness is held together by what the pre-Socratic philosopher Heraclitus called the Logos, the gathering principle, the invisible syntax that binds together God and nature via desire and design. Desire is the syntax of design, God speaking through nature. The role of art is to listen and translate.

That Guy would one day become my mentor was more or less an accident of geography. I grew up in the suburbs of Louisville, Kentucky, and my parents had few books in the house that weren't Bibles or guides to the Christian life. Still, due in part to the encouragement of an English teacher, I decided toward the end of high school that I wanted to be a writer. I applied to several universities with reputations for producing famous writers, but my high school grades were poor, and in the end I was accepted only into my state school, the University of Kentucky. My English teacher told me to make the best of it and to try to take a class with some writer named Guy Davenport.

When I arrived on campus in the fall of 1985, I went to the newsroom of the student paper, the *Kentucky Kernel,* and asked for an assignment. That September, Guy's collection of essays *Every Force Evolves a Form* had been nominated for the National Book Critics Circle Award. But apparently no one on the regular staff of the paper wanted anything to do with that story. They had all heard about this professor's intimidating presence and his caustic attitude toward students.

The editor looked through her file of assignments and asked if I had ever heard of Guy Davenport. I said that I had. She told me to go interview him and write up a profile for the features section of the paper. I went straight to the university library and checked out Guy's first book of stories, *Tatlin!* I could make absolutely no sense of it. I had read Thomas Hardy in high school and thought that rough going, but I had never read anything remotely like this. The sentences were unending, the languages multiple, the allusions beyond me, the plots unrecognizable. And somewhere inside that dense thicket of prose, the characters seemed to be having a lot of sex.

As I recall, the interview in Guy's UK office was something of a disaster. He sat at his desk beneath a portrait he had painted of

James Joyce, chain-smoking Marlboro Reds and batting away my inept questions. After about forty-five minutes, he said that I must certainly have enough information for my article and sent me on my way. Somehow I pulled the story together and eventually got promoted to staff writer at the paper. But it took two years before I screwed up the courage to actually register for one of Guy's classes. While he was calling the roll that first day, he paused over my name and said, "The reporter from the *Kernel*?" I nodded. "I'll remember you," he replied ominously. The whole class turned its pitiable gaze in my direction. You poor bastard, they all seemed to be thinking.

By then, however, I had read a few more of Guy's books. Something I couldn't have named at the time kept pulling me back to their richly layered world. I had become fascinated with early-twentieth-century painting, and slowly I began to see that Guy was translating many of those techniques—particularly collage—into language. I also began to appreciate how sensuous that language appeared, how many *things* grounded the sentences, like sandbags holding down a hot air balloon. If Guy's thinking seemed to rise inevitably into the Pythagorean realm of the abstract, then the sensual, tactile world kept seducing it back to earth:

> Late afternoon, rich coffee, a tobacco smelling of tar and of honey from a cedar hive, a map of Rotterdam on the wall, as Vermeer would have it. Adriaan sipped the sumptuous coffee, smoked the fragrant pipe.

That's Adriaan von Havendaal, the Dutch philosopher Guy invented as an alter ego in his early fiction. But Guy wasn't writing fiction in any conventional, recognizable sense. Instead he was constructing prose assemblages out of philosophy, poetry, natural history, archaeology, mathematics, and a particularly arcane version of the erotic. At times he interspersed these prose hybrids with his own meticulous pen-and-ink drawings.

The course I had signed up for was Comp Lit I. On my first essay, Guy took issue with some of my assertions about cubism but allowed that I had made a few good points. On my second essay, he wrote only: "Promising." At the end of my third essay, he asked if we might get together for "coffee and conversation."

This threw me into a kind of panic. I was a provincial kid from Kentucky. My parents were Sunday school teachers. I didn't speak French, or Italian, or any of the other five languages in which Guy was fluent. On top of that, there were the vague rumors around campus that Guy was gay, perhaps even a pedophile. Despite the obvious fact of his thirty-year relationship with Bonnie Jean Cox, many of Guy's stories take as their subject alliances between boys and older, wiser guardians—or what the *Los Angeles Times* once called "pederastic sex play." That got tongues wagging around campus, especially the tongues of some colleagues who (if you can imagine this in academia) resented Guy's success.

We met for coffee at his house in Bell Court, the oldest suburb in Lexington. Nothing salacious or even very remarkable happened. Guy could sense my nervousness, I think, and he tried to put me at ease by talking about the Southern Baptist upbringings we had in common. His house had a quality about it that the Danish call *hygge,* a word that translates poorly as "coziness." It was cluttered but neat, dark but welcoming. The walls of his living room were covered in burlap instead of wallpaper, but you could barely see it for all of the bookcases and paintings. Even the mantel (and as I later learned, the cupboards) functioned as a bookcase. Two rather worn chairs sat facing each other on either side of the fireplace. We sat there and talked.

Over the next few years, we became friends. Guy would invite me over for coffee—he loved coffee, disapproved of alcohol—and we would spend long Friday afternoons talking, looking at books and paintings, and listening to everything from Mozart to Lead Belly to field recordings of music by the Dogon tribe of Africa. I remember those afternoons as luminous and exciting. I was learning a great deal of things, and of course Guy's attention made me feel that perhaps I too had what it took to be a writer, perhaps I could translate the psychic forces of my own life into a form that might rise to the level of art. If I didn't have any place to be that night, Guy and I would walk a mile to the grocery store and buy the makings for cheeseburgers or bologna sandwiches. On the way back, Guy gathered up fallen branches; "There's free firewood everywhere," he'd say. By the time we reached his house, we both had two armloads of wood—the makings of the evening fire. While it crackled at our feet, we sat and talked some more. And while I don't think it was ever his intention, as we sat before many fires, Guy gradually taught me how to think and how to write.

Other times, if it was a sunny day, Guy painted while we visited. He had made a studio out of a small second-floor room. With windows on three sides, light poured into it, and Guy would sit at his easel in an old wicker chair. He liked to paint portraits of the subjects he was writing about at the time—Heraclitus, Kafka, Kierkegaard, Wittgenstein. As an artist, Guy's style varied wildly. He could paint as sensuously as Modigliani or as severely as Mondrian. Usually he would be working on some geometrical abstraction while we talked. He loved to paint grids ("Grids are good for you," he would say), and he rendered them with a tiny brush as if to savor as long as possible the tactile nature of the work. "Men talk about the world without paying attention to the world, as if they were asleep," wrote Heraclitus. I slowly began to see that in Guy, I had met for the first time someone who was completely awake and alive.

In 1990, Guy was awarded the MacArthur "Genius" Fellowship. No one at the University of Kentucky had ever won a MacArthur. The genius that a few critics had attributed to Guy was suddenly confirmed and certified. The local paper asked what he planned to buy with the prize money. Guy said a few more bottles of Perrier.

I was taking his James Joyce graduate seminar at the time. After class he and I would walk to a nearby deli for lunch. Each day I made a feeble gesture of trying to pay for my sandwich, and each day Guy said, "Oh, we'll let John D. and Catherine T. MacArthur get this one." If it was a nice day, we ate outside on the limestone steps of a campus amphitheater. I remember one week when Guy was puzzling over, as many scholars have, that mysterious sentence Thoreau inserted into *Walden*: "I long ago lost a hound, a bay horse, and a turtledove, and am still on their trail." Guy was rereading all of Mencius because he dimly remembered that the Chinese philosopher had said something similar. This is what he finally found:

> If one loses a fowl or a dog, he knows well how to seek them
> again; if one loses the sentiments of his heart, he does not
> know how to seek them again. The duties of practical phi-
> losophy consists only in seeking after the sentiments of the
> heart which we have lost; that is all.

Thoreau's turtledove and the hound could be found again. But the bay horse—the sentiment of the heart, the laws of one's own nature—that we must seek to recover through what Mencius called a practical philosophy. Guy, I think, applied such a practical philosophy to his own life. Because he found himself so out of place as a bookish child in the South ("I was thought to be retarded," he later wrote), he seemed to give up very early on the prospect of assimilation. Instead he began learning, as he wrote in his essay "On Reading," "the philosophical simpleness that would get me through life." He didn't go to faculty parties because he didn't like small talk. He spent so much time alone because he enjoyed his own company. He didn't own a TV because he would rather read. He didn't drive because he thought the speed and impersonality of the automobile ("a bionic roach") had ruined the modern city that Le Corbusier envisioned. He didn't think there was enough beauty in the world, so he created entire imaginary countries and populated them with artists, philosophers, boy scouts and enlightened scout masters. He lived alone. He had tried marriage, briefly, and the disaster of that entanglement convinced Guy that his DNA had predisposed him to a more solitary habitation. He had consciously chosen that island life, alone in a house full of books and paintings, and it seemed that he knew himself well enough to realize that this was the only life with which he could be satisfied.

Guy thought there were two kinds of genius: one that is cultivated by an enlightened society (think Mozart) and another that God simply drops in the middle of nowhere as a kind of cosmic joke (think Joseph Cornell). Guy's genius was of the latter sort. He grew up in Anderson, South Carolina, surrounded by a family that loved him but could make little of his talent or his very un-southern, solitary nature. As soon as possible, he left for Duke University, then Oxford, then Harvard, with two involuntary military stints in between. While at Harvard, he published in the school literary magazine a couple of short stories that today read like pretty bad imitations of Faulkner. Perhaps sensing this, he quit writing fiction for twenty-four years. And when he returned to it in the early seventies, he was a wholly different writer. When Alfred Corn initiated an interview for the *Paris Review* by characterizing Guy as a southern writer, Guy called a halt to the interview. He even perversely stacked all of his books from floor to ceiling in his living room, then pointed out to Corn, by letter, that exactly six pages of that towering prose took up the South as its subject. Those six pages comprise two stories. One is about a little boy who likes to wear gingham dresses; the other is about the burial of a dove.

Guy was from the South, but he wasn't a southerner; he was raised by Baptists, but he wasn't a Christian. These were things we had in common, and they formed the basis of many long conversations. Guy used to say that he was a "Baptist agnostic"—that is, he didn't believe in the church's promise of eternal salvation, but he was also under no illusion that he could wholly escape its influence. Perhaps as a result of this tension, much of his fiction is a long working out of an alternative theology purged of prudery, doctrine, and boredom. Like the Mediterranean street preacher Yeshua, Guy's two most prominent characters, Adriaan von Havendaal and the Danish scout master Hugo Tvemunding, gather around them people from the margins of their cultures to form a wholly new kind of social unit. Yet unlike Yeshua's followers, Guy's outcasts are mostly children. He viewed childhood as its own kind of utopia, a realm that had been almost completely obliterated by post-Victorian Comstockery. To Guy, the oppression of boys begins at birth, with circumcision, which he viewed as outright mutilation of the body. And Guy agreed with World War I pacifist and progressive Randolph Bourne that the greatest and final failure of that oppression was to march eighteen- and nineteen-year-old boys off to fight a war thought up by old men. Instead, childhood should be a radical, amoral adventure, driven by that most innate of youthful engines, curiosity. In "August Blue," the Henry Scott Tuke painting that hung in Guy's bedroom, three naked boys splash playfully around in a wooden rowboat on the Thames, but behind them, a fleet of battleships looms on the horizon.

Guy's writing was as radical in content as it was beautiful in form. In that, it reminds me of Nietzsche, and perhaps like the philosopher who lived alone in rented rooms, Guy felt the need to retreat, to cloister, to isolate himself from the judgment of his colleagues and his neighbors. In his last published essay, Guy praised the reclusive Chicago "outsider artist" Henry Darger for having "the integrity to work in peaceful solitude from 1912 until his death in 1973." Then Guy added, "Darger lived, richly, in a parallel world that he had to create daily, page by page." And that is where Guy lived as well, for much of his life. In his first book of essays, he gave that realm a name—the geography of the imagination. It was there that Guy made peace with his obsessions.

But why was that imaginary geography populated by so many naked boys? That is often the question that seems to lurk around Guy's work. We know from Doctors Freud and Kinsey that all human sexuality exists along a continuum. Mothers leave their husbands and children for other women; linebackers have involuntary dreams about the quarterback. Guy rejected the labels that Americans obsessively apply to sexuality: homosexual, lesbian, heterosexual, pedophile. He shared Michel Foucault's view, filtered through the ancient Greeks, that standards of moderation are more important than the standardization of sex.

The shrewd critic Wyatt Mason has suggested that all of Guy's fiction is really asking one, persistent question: "What if we were free?" That Guy may have wanted to be free to love boys has made many critics, colleagues, and friends uneasy. One could say that because Guy *wasn't* legally free to love boys, he sublimated his affection through his fiction. And I think that is true, as far as it goes. But it doesn't go far enough. A much larger point needs to be made: Guy believed that attraction is fundamentally amoral. We love what, and who, we love. Period.

Guy found his greatest ally for what we might call this erotic economics in the utopian writings of Charles Fourier, and I think that in an important way, Fourier saved Guy and helped him map out a psychological geography where he didn't feel so alone. Fourier contended that all Western philosophy was rubbish because it ran counter to human nature, trying to make us into something other than who we naturally are. Happiness was the point of life, wrote

Fourier, not virtue, or goodness, or truth. But in pursuit of virtue, we too often repress the natural instincts, which then reappear perversely as malevolence. Far better, said Fourier, to work with, rather than against, the instincts and to organize communities in such a way that individual desires served the general good. In Fourier's utopia of New Harmony, someone with a violent nature was made the butcher. People who liked to lick toes were paired with those who liked their toes licked. And so on. Mania was not a disease but simply an expression of nature's diversity.

By the end of his life, Fourier had decided that only a group of children, uncorrupted by civilization, could make New Harmony work; he even wrote a letter to Napoleon asking to adopt five hundred French orphans. Guy's most ambitious work of fiction, the novel *Apples and Pears,* takes the form of Adriaan von Havendaal's journal from 1981 as the Dutch philosopher sets up a small Fourierist phalanx in the Netherlands (nether land, no land), made up mostly of adolescents and children. When the book was going to press in 1983, Guy panicked, thinking its content—a free love commune where incest and pedophilia were condoned—might get him fired from UK. He tried to withdraw the manuscript, and I have no idea what publisher Jack Shoemaker said to convince Guy that the book should go forward.

The Netherlands of *Apples and Pears* was created wholly out of Guy's imagination, but when he began traveling to Denmark in the eighties, Guy was thrilled to find a culture that looked so much like the imaginary homelands of his later books, *The Jules Verne Steam Balloon* and *The Drummer of the Eleventh North Devonshire Fusilliers.* Of course it might be that Guy simply saw what he wanted to see, a Denmark that aligned with his own expectations. Guy could invent reality as easily and convincingly as he could invent fiction. But what Guy claimed to see was a country of "successful and happy human beings" who "are unembarrassed by the facts of life" and have "decriminalized every affection they can think of." It was no accident to Guy that the Danish scholar Georg Brandes was the first person to lecture on Nietzsche. It was Nietzsche, after all, who had written, "To have to fight the instincts—that is the formula of decadence: as long as life is *ascending,* happiness equals instinct." And it is true that Denmark usually scores highest every year on some new happiness index. Many scholars attribute this to the convivial nature of the Danes, a people who are compulsively social, inveterate joiners of clubs and leagues. Guy, I think, always secretly wanted to be a joiner, but only of the kind of culture he imagined in his fiction, one where he was the benevolent overseer.

This isolated him, and while Guy praised and protected his solitude, I think it must be said that, in the end, there was something missing. Namely, friends. Guy had very few of them. He was lucky, of course, to have found a lifelong companion in Bonnie Jean, with whom he shared dinners, evenings, and vacations. And during the sixties, he seemed to very much value his friendships with the monk Thomas Merton (cloistered nearby in Bardstown, Kentucky) and the photographer Ralph Eugene Meatyard. But by the time I met Guy, both men were dead: Merton accidentally electrocuted in Thailand; Meatyard lost to cancer.

When it first occurred to me that Guy spent so much time as a writer dreaming up communities in which he would have liked to belong, I felt a raw sadness. Friendship is really the dominant theme winding throughout his fiction. Heraclitus said that a friend is another self, and I think Guy was always looking for that elusive true friend, that other self. He had found Thoreau's bay horse, the sentiments of his own heart, but I'm not sure he ever found Thoreau's hound—the true friend. There is a painful passage in the "Wednesday" chapter of *A Week on the Concord and Merrimack Rivers* in which Thoreau writes, "We never exchange more than three words with a Friend in our lives on that level to which our thoughts and feelings almost habitually rise. One goes forth prepared to say, 'Sweet Friends!' and the salutation is, 'Damn your eyes.'" I suspect that this perverse psychology lay behind much of Guy's perceived coldness. He seemed at times to hold Thoreau's nearly impossible standards for friendship. And he felt too vulnerable in his affections to say "Sweet Friend!" so as a result, more than a few people felt the sting of "Damn your eyes!"

There is, in Guy's story "The Jules Verne Steam Balloon," a very revealing, and I think very autobiographical, passage. Hugo Tvemunding's father, a retired minister, is telling Hugo's girlfriend, Mariana,

> I'm wonderfully delighted that you and Hugo are friends. He
> has always been a friendly boy. He used to toddle off behind
> the postman, and grieve that he could not stay longer than to
> hand over the mail and exchange comments on the weather.
> He made friends with the girl who delivered butter and
> eggs. He fell in love with all his schoolmates. He is indeed,
> Mariana said, a very loving person. His loving nature, Pastor
> Tvemunding said, causes him grief from time to time.

I believe the same can be said about Guy. He harbored a deep sensitivity, accompanied by a deep fear of being hurt or misunderstood. What Guy harbored, of course, was the child we all carry within us, but for Guy, the child seemed particularly fragile. To protect himself, to scab over his wounds, Guy often put up a front, and so he often came across as distant and aloof. That, coupled with his natural erudition, often made people uncomfortable. What's more, Guy's default mode of discourse tended to be the long monologue; he talked *at* you. And when you finally responded, he could be very dismissive of what you had to say. This got worse as he got older, and the few friends he did have stopped coming around. I stopped, for the most part, until the very end, when I was needed.

Years later, in his final letter to the poet Lee McCarthy, I found this: "I have Erik Reece hard at work cleaning middens of papers upstairs and down. Erik has just filed about 10,000 recent letters. And cleaned up a bathroom that I was using as an attic annex. Thank God for friends who rally around." It kind of broke me up.

As a teacher, Guy lectured. Or rather he talked for fifty minutes in elliptical patterns, moving from one subject to the next much like an electron. Sometimes Guy would draw arrows back and forth on the chalkboard, from Vico to da Vinci to Samuel Beckett to Buster Keaton. But more often, he just leaned against the board, rolled a piece of chalk back and forth across the palm of his right hand, and talked. Rarely did he speak directly to whatever text we happened to be reading. Comp Lit I went on like this for eight weeks until one day Guy suddenly asked the class, "Who here has read *The Kreutzer Sonata* by Tolstoy?" I was stupid enough to raise my hand. "What's it about, Erik?" he asked. My mind went blank. "It's about sex, Erik, the story is about sex." Unimpressed with that failed attempt at class participation, Guy lectured on for the rest of the semester. We all took notes, but God knows what sense we made of them afterward.

Guy always returned our essays the class period after we turned them in. They were neatly creased down the middle, and on the back was a generally low grade with a one- or two-word explanation. Still, when the roles were reversed at the end of the semester, and more than a few students gave him low marks on course evaluations, he always seemed wounded, genuinely aggrieved. Gradually Guy came to see himself as a failed teacher. But he wasn't. I think the failure was more on our part, as students. Too many of us lacked that one thing Guy thought so vital to education—curiosity. If we couldn't *see* what an amazing movement modernism was in the history of literature and art, what more could he do? He told anecdotes about meeting T. S. Eliot and Samuel Beckett, Ezra Pound and

William Carlos Williams. He had personally tracked down some of the most important artists of the twentieth century. He could tell us firsthand what they had said about the nature of art in the modern world. If we couldn't get excited about that, what were we doing in Comp Lit I? The sad truth is that most of us probably didn't even know. Friends like Hugh Kenner and John Barth urged Guy to leave UK, to move on to a more prestigious school, where his expertise would be better appreciated. But Guy had hunkered down at 621 Sayre Avenue, where the fashionable literati and the salons could not find him, and that's the way he liked it. He would continue to make the half-hour walk to UK, chain-smoke Marlboros in his office, deliver his two lectures for the day, and head back home to write.

Guy hated pretense, and it could bring out a real strain of anti-intellectualism in him. I remember one night when a prominent American poet came to give a reading in Lexington and requested Guy's presence at dinner. (I was there as his driver.) This poet and Guy had been at Harvard together in the fifties, and the poet's erudition was on full display. He quoted medieval philosophers, he switched from one language to the next, he dismissed Walter Benjamin as overrated. I could tell Guy was recoiling at this public immodesty. At a break in one of these soliloquies, Guy piped up and said, "Hey, has anybody seen the new *Harry Potter* movie?" The prominent American poet looked aghast. We soon left.

Guy was never about status or career or fame or reputation. He never went on a book tour or exhibited any of his paintings. He hated everything related to the notion of *self*. I don't mean that he hated himself but rather that he hated the American cult of self, and he especially hated the role of the writer as prophet. He found it all unseemly and would quote Menander as saying, "Talking about oneself is a feast that starves the guest." The natural world, the world of art and literature, the human mind and body—these things were so fascinating, why waste time talking about oneself?

There was something both refreshing and terrifying about how Guy always said exactly what he was thinking. Once, on a flight to Paris, a French flight attendant asked Guy how his coffee was. He replied, "It tastes like vacuum cleaner dust stirred around in tepid water." This so amused the flight attendant that she fetched Guy a complimentary bottle of port. But he could be cruelly honest in his judgment of your work. When a neighbor who had spent two years in prison for refusing to fight in Vietnam showed Guy the poems he had written while incarcerated, Guy told him unceremoniously that he had no talent for poetry and should go back to protesting the war. Once, when I showed him a chapter of what I thought might be a novel, he replied, "Jesus Christ, I didn't know you wanted to be John Updike." It was, I'm quite sure, the meanest thing he could think to say. While I was living in Virginia, Guy and I kept up a steady correspondence, and his letters often included some kind of hand-painted collage. I tried once to reciprocate by sending him my colored-pencil rendering of a prairie warbler. He wrote back: "You draw like a talented third-grader." But when you wrote something good, Guy told you that as well. When he would praise a poem of mine, I knew I could trust that judgment; I knew the poem must be alright.

Guy didn't take up causes. Unlike his UK colleague Wendell Berry, who puts reform at the heart of his work, Guy thought American consumer culture was beyond reform. He told me once that he gave up on American politics when Eisenhower beat Adlai Stevenson for president in 1956 (Guy had worked as a graduate assistant for Archibald MacLeish, who at the time was writing speeches for Stevenson). He spoke with bemused detachment about campus idealism during "the glorious '60s." And though he reviewed books for the right-wing *National Review,* he did so simply because Hugh Kenner got him the job, not because he felt any allegiance to William F. Buckley or the conservative movement. He was surprised to open the *National Review* in 1968 and see his name included in a full-page ad that announced: "Writers for Nixon." He hadn't been asked for the endorsement, he didn't vote for Nixon, but neither did he bother to clear up the confusion. When the poet C. K. Williams wrote to say that he was burning all Guy's books because of the Nixon endorsement, Guy rolled his eyes and threw the letter on the evening's fire.

There was also some whispering from time to time that Guy had anti-Semitic tendencies because of his allegiance to Ezra Pound. This is simply nonsense. It was precisely because of the Holocaust that Guy never allowed his books to be translated into German. Moreover, one of Guy's great heroes was the Polish pediatrician and educator Janusz Korczak, who ran an orphanage in pre–World War II Warsaw. Korczak exposed the children to the challenges of real life, and the orphans took on more and more responsibility until they gradually formed a kind of children's republic within the orphanage. Korczak also wrote a novel called *King Matt the First* about a child king who rallies both children and adults around a constitution of trust and cooperation. But in the cruelest of ironies, it was the barbaric adults of the Third Reich who sent all 192 of Korczak's Jewish orphans to be murdered at Treblinka. Korczak, a non-Jew who wanted nothing to do with that adult world, accompanied his wards to his own voluntary death in the gas chambers. One day, when Guy was recounting this story to our Comp Lit I class, he broke down in tears and staggered out of the room.

Guy kept smoking right up to the last. "I'm operating on the assumption that I cannot get cancer," he said after the diagnosis had been confirmed. The last time I saw Guy, a few days before he died, he was sitting by his fireplace, wrapped up in a thick red blanket. He was cold, shivering, unshaven, weak as a kitten. He didn't want to talk because if he did, he would start coughing and wouldn't be able to stop. He dozed by the fire. I rearranged logs, moved stacks of paper, paced. He would open his eyes from time to time to see that I was still there, then close them again. There was a strange kind of understanding in his tired gaze: "You are here. I am dying. This is it."

In the years following Guy's death, people would occasionally ask me, "What was Guy *really* like?" I think, in part, what they were asking was, "What was Guy like when he wasn't holding forth on some matter of high art, when he wasn't lording his great intellect over you?" But that's who Guy was in public as well as in front of his fire. That part of his nature wasn't false or meant to create distance. He was simply, as he liked to quote Lincoln, "interested in the things he was interested in." His interests and his curiosity were so vast, it sometimes looked like demagoguery, but it wasn't.

Having said that, I think there were at least five Guy Davenports. There was the man who wrote some of the most beautiful prose in our country's history. There was the lively, congenial writer of letters. There was the erudite professor whose fifty-minute lectures usually covered at least three thousand years of human history. There was the man who talked with his few friends in front of his fireplace. And then there was the mysterious, utterly private man that no one knew. I do not know, of course, how future scholars will judge Guy's work and his life. But I do know that such judgment is something Guy cared nothing about. I return, again and again, to Bonnie Jean's statement about the innocence of Guy's mind. Guy's affections were purified by their innocence, and I believe his soul ascended out of his battered flesh with lightness and grace.

INSTEAD OF THE TEN COMMANDMENTS

I n my home state of Kentucky, college basketball is our religion. We all know it and we all agree upon it, at least tacitly. Our catechism begins, "On, on, U of K, we are right for the fight today," and ends, "We will kick, pass. and run 'til the victory is won." Granted, it's no "Song of David," but the steady time signature can keep huge crowds plowing along on roughly the same beat. It binds us together in acts of vicarious catharsis, a solidarity that I take to be the point, more or less, of organized religion.

So earlier this fall, when a grassroots movement began in Corbin, Kentucky, to introduce a bill before the state legislature that would require the Ten Commandments to be posted in public buildings, I simply took it as testament to the fact that basketball season hadn't begun. But here it is December, the Kentucky Wildcats are 3–0, and still the Ten Commandments are popping up on classroom and courtroom walls in Pulaski, McCreary, and Harlan County.

The Kentucky General Assembly passed the same bill into law back in 1978, only to have it struck down by the US Supreme Court two years later. But decades have passed, and last week a sizable religious contingent took to the steps of the state capitol, rallying again for public display of Mosaic Law. When I turned on the news, I saw teenagers wearing what looked like sandwich boards, each one embossed with one of the commandments. The girl who stood closest to the camera was holding a placard that read in large block letters: THOU SHALL NOT WORSHIP ANY GRAVEN IMAGES. I wondered: When was the last time anybody even saw, much less worshipped, a graven image? The images we worship these days are the opposite of graven; they are created by pixels—images of celebrities, or people who want to be celebrities, endlessly reproduced on the screens of our TVs and electronic devices. And while I would argue that worshipping these images does pose serious problems for American adolescents, that's not why the schools and courthouses of eastern Kentucky were filling up with the Ten Commandments.

So let me move on to the other commandments. As for the latter half of the Decalogue, there usually isn't much objection, even from the most strident antichurch quarters. Commandments six, eight, and nine (killing, stealing, perjuring) offer undeniably good advice for anyone who wants to stay out of jail. In my state—and I don't think Kentuckians are unique this way—disregarding the tenth commandment about your neighbor's wife is a good way to get yourself killed. And conversely, being faithful to one's spouse (number seven) can prevent a lot of heartache all around. In the word of Pulaski County judge-executive Darrell BeShears, these later proscriptions are just "good rules to live by."

No, it's really the first few commandments that ultimately get the attention of the chief justices. In fact, the first commandment presents such a theological and political snare that a serious thinker might never even move on to the second. *Thou shalt have no other gods before me* has always troubled theologians, seeing as it catches the one-and-only-God admitting to the existence of other gods. And that, of course, is the real problem. About 15 percent of "other" Americans—"other" being the statistical category to which they are usually relegated—believe in other gods. Or in no gods. Or in goddesses. Or pagan spirits. And therefore, out of respect for every citizen's religious liberty, the First Amendment bars the state from endorsing or enforcing—from *establishing*—a particular religious point of view. Such is the ACLU's argument whenever it is summoned (in McCreary County it was contacted by the judge-executive's own cousin) to mount a legal defense for civil liberties.

But personally, I have another problem with the Ten Commandments: they simply aren't all that inspiring. After all, what student or citizen was ever stirred to intellectual creativity, much less self-realization, by a list of ten things he or she cannot do? It's a low bar, a dreary set of prohibitions by a god who doesn't seem to put much trust in his chosen people. It seems to say: If you can't be good, at least don't be bad. Good advice for a penal colony, perhaps, but not for the one democratic institution—public schools—where we put our hope and faith in the generations to come.

I would like, therefore, to propose that another set of injunctions be hung publicly as an alternative to the Ten Commandments. This credo is at once inclusively and uniquely American. I am speaking of Walt Whitman's poem "Laws for Creations," which goes as follows:

LAWS for Creations,
For strong artists and leaders, for fresh broods of teachers and
    perfect literats for America,
For noble savans and coming musicians.

All must have reference to the ensemble of the world, and the
    compact truth of the world,
There shall be no subject too pronounced—all works shall
    illustrate the divine law of indirections.

What do you suppose Creation is?

What do you suppose will satisfy the Soul, except to walk free and
own no superior?

What do you suppose I would intimate to you in a hundred ways, but
that man or woman is as good as God?

And that there is no God any more divine than Yourself?

And that is what the oldest and newest myths finally mean?

And that you or any one must approach Creations through such laws?

This poem has a lot to recommend it. "Laws for Creations" is shorter than the Ten Commandments, for one thing. And Whitman's penchant for repetition makes it easy to memorize. More importantly, it never mentions the word *not*. This is significant, because whereas the Ten Commandments obviously fell from the Tree of the Knowledge of Good and Evil, Whitman derives his laws from the other, neglected Tree of Life, which also stood in the middle of the early paradise.

From the Tree of Good and Evil, we learned to *judge* the world, and to judge each other. It was only after Adam and Eve ate from this tree that they felt shame about their nakedness. When Yahweh found them stitching together fig-leaf loincloths, He asked why, and Adam responded, "Because I was naked." That's how Yahweh knew the first humans had eaten from the forbidden tree: they spoke a new language—the language of judgment.

Before that, they spoke only a poetry of naming. When Yahweh bestowed upon Adam and Eve the task of conferring names upon all the beasts of the garden, He allowed them to take part in the mystery of creation, making words out of the same substance— *pneuma*, breath—with which He had called the world into being. But saddled with the new knowledge of good and evil, Adam and Eve abdicated their role as poets and became, to Yahweh's great disgust, *critics*.

Consider the telling comment that Yahweh makes to the angels after he finds the primordial parents dressed up in fig leaves: "Man has become like one of us, he knows good and evil" (3:22). Such an extraordinary admission actually allows us to answer Western philosophy's most foundational question: "Why is there something instead of nothing?" That is to say, why does the world exist in the first place? The answer, we learn here, is that Yahweh wanted to create a world that would operate *outside* the knowledge of good and evil—a world without judgment. There is no other accounting for his single, arbitrary prohibition against eating from the second tree.

Yahweh must have grown bored with his own dry realm of unchanging, infallible laws. In the middle of a brilliant legal career, Yahweh realized one day that He hated his job as high judge, ultimate arbiter. So He set up a potter's wheel in the shed out back and spun the universe into being. It was a work of art, a world where beauty trumped law and desire was the syntax of design. Which is to say, it was a very Whitmanesque kind of place. And that is the ontological and theological realm Whitman calls us back to in "Laws for Creations." If we turn our attention back to the Tree of Life, he urges, we might begin to understand how the natural laws *of this world*—"the divine laws of indirections"—are synonymous with the laws of the Creator.

It was a tenet of transcendentalism—the antinomian American religion that Ralph Waldo Emerson invented and Whitman readily embraced—that the natural world is a scripture we can translate if only we pay close enough attention. (In another poem, Whitman called the flowering world "a realm of budding bibles.") What we need, say Emerson and Whitman, is already here. For Emerson, the study of nature is a religious sacrament because we come to know the Creator through the creation. What's more, we come to understand the correspondence between the natural world and our own true natures. We see that both are the work of one Creator, and we see that the kingdom without is reflected by a kingdom within. That later kingdom is our evidence—all we need, said Emerson—that we still carry within us a divine spark, an ember of the world's original light. And for that reason, said Whitman, we can walk free and own no superior. We can trust that all true acts of inspiration come of that freedom—what Emerson called instinct and spontaneity—a freedom cut loose from the doctrine and dogma of dying institutions. In the end, transcendentalism created its own kind of trinity whereby to study nature is to study the self and to study the self is to discover one's one divine nature.

When Whitman assures us in "Laws for Creations" that "there is no God any more divine than Yourself," he is confirming Emerson's intuition that we still carry within ourselves a portion of that original, divine light. He is saying that the laws of Yahweh-the-artist manifest themselves in the laws of his creation and that they consequently become the laws of the heart. "And that is what the oldest and newest myths finally mean." Indeed, in the world's oldest religious scriptures, the Vedas of India, we do find this ancient idea:

> The individual self, deluded by forgetfulness of his identity with the divine Self, bewildered by his ego, grieves and is sad. But when he recognizes the worshipful Lord as his own true Self, and beholds his glory, he grieves no more.

[trans. Swami Prabhavananda and Frederick Manchester]

This notion of God as a creative force dwelling within each of us seems to me much more inspired and inspiring than the idea of God as a judge who constantly watches us through a surveillance camera that we have internalized, a crippling mechanism that William Blake called the "mind-forged manacles." Unlike the Ten Commandments, "Laws for Creations" doesn't tell us what we cannot do; rather it tells us what we can. It calls us to our higher selves.

It calls us to be artists of our own lives. It calls us to be statesmen instead of politicians, makers not of mere commodities but of genuine, enduring artifacts, teachers who inspire in students a sense of self-cultivation—"the unfolding of [one's] nature," which Emerson called, "the chief end of man."

Right now our students are too often the acolytes of the vacuous images that move across their screens and dominate so much of their mental theater. I see this in my own students, and as a result they are often hesitant to stand apart, to appear different, to speak from the heart. If hung in the homerooms of American public schools, "Laws for Creations" would urge them to look away from the virtual world that technology has surrounded them with and to look within themselves for sources of their own individual character. "Laws for Creations" would urge them to act as magnanimously as men and women who still carry within themselves a vestige of the divine. Imagine schoolchildren beginning each day on that ennobling thought.

BIRDING WITH WENDELL BERRY

I t is eight in the morning on the last day of the world. We are standing, six of us, alongside the county road that cuts across Wendell Berry's farm in the small Kentucky town of Port Royal. To our right, the Kentucky River has retreated back inside its banks after a tempestuous spring. In the lower pasture, a single llama guards Wendell's sheep against coyotes. Up on the hill to our left stands the Berrys' traditional white farmhouse as well as several busily occupied martin houses. The birds are what bring us here each May, but radio preacher Harold Camping's doomsday prediction that the world will end tomorrow, May 21, has lent today a kind of cosmic, I mean comic, significance.

"Well," Wendell says, wearing khaki work pants and a team sweatshirt from one of his granddaughters' high schools, "if this is our last day, we might as well have as much fun as we can."

"No better place to do that," says botanist Bill Martin, and we all nod our agreement. Besides Bill, our coterie includes wildlife biologists John Cox and Joe Guthrie, me, Wendell, and his retired neighbor Harold Tipton. Wendell, Bill, and Harold are of one generation; John, Joe, and I are of another. Some semblance of this group has been congregating here for the past ten years. The official nature of our business is to count and identify birds—migratory warblers and summer residents. But our pursuits might better be described in terms of what Wendell calls a "scientific quest for conversation." As much as anything, we come to hear and tell stories.

Wendell has been telling the story of this land for five decades. A few hundred yards upstream from where we have gathered stands his writing studio, an approximately twelve-by-sixteen-foot room that overlooks the river and was the subject of a defining early essay, "The Long-Legged House." Sitting atop long stilts, the "camp," as Wendell calls the studio, slightly resembles a great blue heron standing silently on the riverbank. It has no electricity, but natural light flows in through a large window, over a long desk where Wendell has written more than fifty books of poetry, fiction. and nonfiction and in the process has become known as the country's leading writer on the subjects of conservation and land stewardship. "It is a room as timely as the body," Wendell wrote in a recent poem,

> As frail, to shelter love's eternal work
> Always unfinished, here at water's edge,
> The work of beauty, faith, and gratitude
> Eternally alive in time.

In tumultuous and uncertain times, it is worth being reminded that these fine things—beauty, faith, gratitude—still lurk eternally beneath history's dark veneer and that an artist working alone in a room beside a river may catch a glimpse of them and render them into a lyric poem, a short story, or an essay.

Because of that work, President Obama awarded Wendell the 2010 National Humanities Medal at a White House ceremony. As he was presenting the award, the president told Wendell that reading his poetry had helped improve his own writing. It is an impressive remark, given that Obama is one of the best writers, along with Jefferson, Lincoln, and Grant, that we've ever had as president.

Perhaps because the camp hovers just beneath the canopy of riverbank trees, the avian world has long been a source and subject of Wendell's poetry. In one poem he writes of seeing a yellow-throated warbler on the railing of his camp porch: "My mind became beautiful/by the sight of him." In Wendell's long series of Sabbath Poems, written on Sunday walks around the farm, birds hover like the constantly circling martins in his front yard:

> It is the Sabbath of the birds
> that so moves me. They belong
> in their ever-returning song, in their flight,
> in their faith in the upholding air,
> to the Original World. They are above us
> and yet of us, for those who fly
> fall, like those who walk.

The "fall" Wendell writes of here is the fall into death, not the fall of man. Indeed, one of the theologies behind the Sabbath Poems is that we still belong to the Original World, if we could only see it that way. But our deeply divided minds have set us off from the natural world and have led us to build all matter of industrial and technological barriers between the two. Standing in contrast to that attitude, and to the attitudes of mainstream Christianity, Wendell long ago called himself a "forest Christian"—one who finds his religion here in this unroofed church, here in "the whole Creation." Thus the poem "Wild Geese" ends with these chthonic lines:

> And we pray, not
> for new earth or heaven, but to be
> quiet in heart, and in eye
> clear. What we need is here.

Such a sentiment points us to a place—spiritually, psychologically, geographically—to begin thinking about how the root of the word *ethic* (the Greek *ethos*) means "dwelling place." As both Ralph Waldo Emerson and Martin Heidegger noted in their respective treatises on poetry, the job of the modern poet is to call us back into that experience of ethical, meaningful dwelling. "My purpose," wrote Wendell, "is a language that can make us whole." The opposite of wholeness is separation, which Martin Luther King Jr. once called our most modern and most troublesome sin. And in many ways, we still remain very estranged from our native landscapes, our neighbors, our government, and the sources of our most basic needs. Emerson wrote that the poet's task is to "re-attach things to nature and the whole." In Emerson's time, Walt Whitman most successfully forged these associations; in contemporary America, our greatest poet of reattachment is Wendell Berry. His purpose is a language that can make us whole as a land community, a human community, and as the community of organisms that we sometimes call the self.

For today's birding, we load into Wendell's pickup and drive a few miles to Harold's farm. A green heron is wading in the creek that runs alongside the road. John and Joe, who are the group's best birders, identify the songs of thrashers, kingbirds, and water thrushes as we pass through these lower reaches. Then Wendell's reluctant truck climbs a nearly washed-out road until we pull into a field in front of a log cabin, hewed out of large oak logs in the 1800s. Wendell's wife, Tanya, and Harold's wife, Edna, have sent along lunch for us. Harold stows our provisions inside the cabin, and the six of us, each armed with a pair of binoculars, set off through high grass and occasional ironweed. Phoebes, towhees, and prairie warblers are singing in the trees at the edge of this meadow. Joe records their names in a small notebook. Having no destination, only this will to wander, we move slowly. "To come in among these trees you must leave behind/ the six days' world," wrote Wendell in a Sabbath Poem, and we have done just that. What's more, Wendell announces that in response to our culture of instant messaging, he has just founded a new cause, the Slow Communication Movement. Certainly we embody that spirit today, and it feels good. It is a more leisurely, more deliberate form of communication, and it isn't limited to 140 characters.

At seventy-seven, Wendell is unapologetically out of fashion, though there really never was a time when this wasn't true. His friend, writer Ed McClanahan, tells the story that years ago, when Wendell's agent called excitedly to say that Robert Redford was giving as Christmas presents copies of Wendell's landmark book *The Unsettling of America*, Wendell turned to Tanya and said, "Queeny, who the hell is Robert Redman?" He famously doesn't own a computer and has written all of his books in longhand.

And yet, after the economic collapse of 2008, Rob Dreher of the *Dallas Morning News* wrote a long column arguing that, in such a moment of crisis, it was finally time we listened to, of all people, Wendell Berry. It was Wendell, he argued, who "stood steadfastly for fidelity to family and community, self-sufficiency, localism, conservation and, above all, learning to get by decently within natural limits"—in other words, all the things that could have staved off a financial crisis driven by rapaciousness and centralized power. The point here is that progress doesn't move inexorably in one direction, toward a technological future, and it doesn't always *look* like progress. In an age of toxic agribusiness and climate crisis, it might look more like a family farm powered by sunlight.

We stop at a lone honey locust standing in the middle of the field, and Wendell calls our attention to its mildly fragrant catkins. Bill holds up a small magnifying glass to the tiny flowers. Such is the nature of this outing—trying to pay attention to the things most of us ignore or simply don't take the time to notice in our daily comings and goings. We must aspire to "the brotherhood of eye and leaf," as Wendell wrote in another poem. To *see* the natural world, after all, either through a magnifying glass or a poem, is the first step toward wanting to preserve it. John points to a song in the crown of the tree and says, "Flycatcher." Joe writes that down.

We walk on, past a thicket where two male indigo buntings, flashing like the bluest shards of stained glass, duel over a female hidden in the brush. Then we stop to watch an orchard oriole (much rarer than the Baltimore variety) perched above the swirling buntings. Wendell is speculating on the brain of a bird, on what a bird can know. "It has the intelligence to adjust its archetype to its place," he finally decides.

"You mean its environment," says Bill.

"I don't use that word," Wendell replies. "It's an abstraction. It separates the organism from its place, and there is no such place."

"Well what do you say then?" demands Bill, who like to needle Wendell.

"I name an actual place. I say Harold Tipton's farm."

It was in fact this attention to the particular that prompted our first walkabout. Eight years ago, Dave Maehr, my colleague at the University of Kentucky, suggested to Wendell that he should catalog all the migratory songbirds that passed through his farm each spring. Wendell liked the idea very much, and we spent the first few years walking those wooded slopes and fields, set only a few miles from where Wendell was born in 1934.

His father was a country lawyer who helped start the Burley Tobacco Growers Cooperative Association during the Depression—an act that was instrumental in keeping small farmers on their land. In 1958 Wendell went off to Stanford to study writing with Wallace Stegner. Then in 1962 he accepted a teaching position at New York University. After a few years in the city, he was ready to come home, back to Henry County. Friends in New York advised him against it; they said returning to Kentucky would be literary suicide. "But I never doubted that the world was more important to me than the literary world," Wendell wrote in his early essay "A Native Hill," and so he and Tanya bought Lanes Landing Farm in 1965. Wendell worked the farm with draft horses, raising cattle, and later Cheviot sheep.

Back in Kentucky, Wendell wrote, "I began to see, however dimly, that one of my ambitions, perhaps my governing ambition, was to belong fully to this place, to belong as the thrushes and the herons and the muskrats belong, to be altogether at home here." One way we humans have found to belong to a place is to tell the story of that place: the story of both its inhabitation and its preservation. Indeed, to walk these woods and fields with Wendell is to traverse an intensely *storied* landscape. The oral tradition overlays this ground like a richly textured matting of fallen leaves. When we walk this land with Wendell, I often think of the Australian aboriginals who compel themselves to *sing* their native landscape as they pass through it. The Australian natives *have* to sing that land, call it again and again into existence, into the present. Those song lines are not so different from Wendell's stories or poems, which have risen up from his own native ground.

One year, as we passed through an abandoned barn, Wendell told us about two brothers who many years ago took over an adjacent family farm after their parents died. They stopped by this barn early one evening when Wendell was about to head up to the house to eat, so he invited them to join him.

"No, Wendell, we already had our dinner," one of the brothers said. "We have to eat early since we don't have enough food for a hungry man."

"Jesus," David said laughing, "where did they get stuff like that."

"It was native intelligence," Wendell replied. "They were men who had never been exposed to radio or TV or the language of the mass media. So they spoke their own kind of poetry."

That year, at the peak of the neotropical warbler migration, we counted more than one hundred different birds. Each year Dave

Maehr would type up the list and send a copy to Wendell, who in turn encouraged Dave to take up a more activist stance toward irresponsible logging practices in Kentucky. Dave responded and in doing so made some enemies within his own forestry department at UK. As a wildlife biologist, he studied large mammals, or "charismatic megafauna," of which Dave was certainly one demonstrative example. He was brash and voluble and generally considered the country's leading expert on the Florida panther. I could tell that Wendell found him to be very good company.

I too found Dave and Wendell and John and Joe and Harold and Bill to be very good company. They were all men who spend much of their time, both at work and at leisure, outdoors, by choice. In that, they represent a kind of American male who is disappearing. These were all independent thinkers, family men, stand-up guys. Their company felt genuine, unforced, natural. They knew the names of things, *real* things, like shumard oaks and bottlebrush grass. They could reattach names to things and in doing so bring themselves closer to the elemental world, make it seem a more inhabitable place. No one carried a cell phone, and no one was in a hurry to be any other place but where we were. No one talked about what he was *feeling*, but I think we all had an unspoken feeling of attachment to one another.

Then, one Sunday morning a month after our fourth excursion to Wendell's, I picked up the Lexington paper to read that Dave was dead. He had been down in Florida, conducting an aerial survey of black bears, when his single-engine plane stalled, then nose-dived, killing Dave and his pilot instantly. As with most sudden deaths, I couldn't quite register what I was reading, couldn't square it with my subjective reality, where Dave was still in the world. We were all stunned, and John, his student and best friend, certainly took it the hardest. A few months later, Wendell wrote me a letter suggesting that we could best honor Dave's memory by continuing our annual avian rite of spring and that we should give it a name: the Dave Maehr Memorial Bird Walk.

So here we are, this time up at Harold's farm, honoring Dave with our peripatetic ritual of walking the fields and forests of central Kentucky. It reminded me of another passage from one of Wendell's poems:

> There are no unsacred places;
> there are only sacred places
> and desecrated places.

This seems to me the fundamental premise undergirding all of Wendell's work—that the natural world is sacred, not a "resource" to be desecrated by the extractive industries that fuel our entire economy. For more than forty years, Wendell has been telling Americans than we cannot survive the economist's dream of infinite economic growth on a finite planet. And certainly some have listened. *The Unsettling of America* redirected the way we think about food and agriculture in this country to the point that the farmer's market is currently the fastest growing part of the American food economy. But obviously not enough people have listened, and so Wendell keeps writing his jeremiads against industrial hooliganism and keeps writing poems that accomplish what philosopher Martin Heidegger called the role of poetry—to praise the whole in the midst of the unholy. I've often thought that Wendell's version of the whole and the holy can be found in this distilled, four-line Sabbath Poem:

> The incarnate Word is with us,
> is still speaking, is present
> always, yet leaves no sign
> but everything that is.

For Wendell, the present is always a window into the eternal moment of the Original World. The natural world is an immanent scripture; how could it not be?

Our meanderings take us down an old logging road shaded by shumard oak and ash trees—"a timbered choir," as Wendell once wrote. Bill is telling a joke that involves farm boys and amorous sheep. When he gets to the punch line, Wendell's laughter crescendos all around us, and I remember something the poet Jane Kenyon once said—that Wendell laughing is "the best noise in the world."

That might come as a surprise to readers of Wendell's polemical tracts, where humor is seldom on display. But Wendell, better than any activist I know, seems to balance his justified sense of outrage at the industrial economy with the pleasure that he takes in the natural world he is fighting to preserve, and in the stories that perpetuate the human comedy.

The first year I came along on the walk, I felt anxious because I wasn't nearly as good a birder as Wendell and the others. We were crossing a stream on Wendell's farm when he suddenly turned to me, pointed skyward, and said, "You hear that, Erik?"

"Uh, well, I'm not sure, uh . . . what is it?"

"That's the hairy-chested nut scratcher!" he said, then slapped his thigh in a burst of laughter.

Now we dip farther down into an older forest, walking among spleenwort ferns and may apples. The birds have grown quieter as the morning stretches out, and Wendell has turned his attention from the sky to the ground. He bends down, brushes away some leaf cover, and starts digging with one hand. "Look how rich this soil is," he remarks, then glances up as the rest of us watch him dig. "The way these old abused hills have been reforested is inexhaustibly interesting to me."

The trees and the ferns and the wildflowers have formed a reciprocal community here on this hillside, based on natural laws that
Wendell calls "mutualistic." Nothing lives here in isolation.

"That's the problem with modern science," Wendell begins,
rising up. "It isolates a problem and offers an isolated solution. To
the problem of depleted soil it offers nitrogen fertilizer. And the
problem with that is a huge dead zone in the Gulf of Mexico because of all that nitrogen runoff."

Conversely, the solution to that botched solution is to better observe the workings of the natural world, to *understand* nature as
measure. For that reason, Wendell often points to the visionary experiments of his friend Wes Jackson, who at the Land Institute in
Salina, Kansas, is creating a new kind of perennial agriculture that
mimics the workings of the midwestern prairie—that holds soil in
place and needs no chemical fertilizers or pesticides.

"Look at all this," Wendell says, standing and gesturing to the
trees. "This isn't wild. This is domestic. What's wild is what's out of
control. That's what we mean by wild. And *we* are the ones that are
out of control. We are the ones creating that dead zone."

Wendell probably knows he is preaching to the converted, but he
also probably knows that one reason we come down each spring is
to hear what's on his mind. Of course, because of such talk, critics
have often dismissed Wendell's writing as "naive" or "unrealistic."
He knows this well enough and has a ready reply for defenders of
the status quo: The word *inevitable* is for cowards.

It is nearing noon and Joe's list has reached almost sixty. We start
back toward the cabin, where Harold, a relentlessly generous man,
soon has a pot of barbecue simmering. We heap portions of it onto
sandwiches, then take our seats around a table in the center of the
cabin's one room.

The barbecue is delicious, the company fine, the weather perfect.
All of this seems to inspire Wendell to reveal his plans to found

another subversive cabal: the Society for the Preservation of Tangibility. The tangible—that which has actual form and substance. In a culture of avatars, electronic friends, and financial "products" that have no basis in reality, such a fundamentally human society sounds attractive indeed.

We all immediately ask if we can join. "Anyone can join," Wendell replies. "There are no dues, no meetings, no fund drives, no newsletter." There is only a state of mind, a desire to preserve what's authentic, what holds substance, what aspires to the whole.

The possibility that a broken world can be made whole seems to be what calls Wendell down to his riverside desk every day. "A man cannot despair," he once wrote, "if he can imagine a better life, and if he can enact something of its possibility." To imagine—it is perhaps the most powerful moral force we possess because it maps a future that is worth finding. It has been Wendell's life's work.

Outside the cabin door, a Carolina wren starts to sing.

A WEEK ON THE KENTUCKY RIVER READING HENRY DAVID THOREAU'S *A WEEK ON THE CONCORD AND MERRIMACK RIVERS*, WHICH NOBODY READS ANYMORE (BUT SHOULD)

> . . . *rivers*
> *Are the Almighty's joy. How could He otherwise*
> *Descend?*
>
> —Friederich Hölderlin

SATURDAY

ALONE ON A mild summer day, I slide my wooden boat down a muddy bank and it lands with a splash in the slack water of the Kentucky River. I scramble down, take a seat at the mid-thwart of this sixteen-foot dory, then pull out onto the heart of the river. Steep walls of limestone stretch along the banks, patrolled by pairs of kingfishers apportioned at half-mile intervals. Often they answer the call of my creaking oarlocks with their own giddy rattle, then sweep around my boat in wide reconnoitering loops, flying inches from the surface of the water. Soon I settle into the familiar, satisfying rhythms that marry arms and oars in a single understanding of wood, water, wind, and bone. I have come down to the Kentucky from my house a few miles upland with a specific task in mind: to spend a week on the river reading, for the fifth or sixth time, Henry David Thoreau's first book, *A Week on the Concord and Merrimack Rivers*. In 1839 Thoreau and his older brother, John, built a boat that they rowed from their home in Concord, Massachusetts, to the source of the Merrimack River near Concord, New Hampshire. Thoreau subsequently wrote a book about the trip—a book that first inspired me to build my own boat. Thoreau called *A Week* an "unroofed book" and said that he hoped it didn't smell of the study or the poet's attic but rather of the fields and woods. Some of his favorite fields and woods ran along the banks of the Concord River, and very similar flora and fauna grow up around the Kentucky, my own native river.

At one point I thought of actually retracing the Thoreau brothers' trip, but last summer I learned an important object lesson concerning the act of pilgrimage. After driving northeast for nearly a thousand miles to make the appropriate displays of reverence at Walden Pond, I pulled up to the park entrance only to find a sign that read: PARKING CAPACITY—FULL. I had made my solemn pilgrimage to the site of Thoreau's solitary utopia—and it was too crowded to even get in. The lesson I took away is this: We need to find our own sacred spaces. Why was Walden Pond, or the Concord and Merrimack Rivers, any more worthy than my own local body of water? Why not read Thoreau's unroofed book here on my own unroofed river? So that is what I set out to do.

I decided I would read one chapter each day for a week to see if I might *experience* the book in a fundamentally different way if I read it in a boat, on a river, under a roofless sky. I could say that I was conducting some kind of thought experiment into the field of neo-Romantic pastoral hermeneutics (if such a thing exists), but really I just wanted to spend part of my summer vacation floating on the Kentucky River, watching the kingfishers and rereading my favorite book.

If you polled a selection of writers and serious readers, I suspect you'd find that a great many have one book they return to again and again, one book that is always near the nightstand, one book that compels them for reasons even they might not wholly understand. It is the book into which they have pasted images, commentaries, and butterfly wings. And often, I would wager, it is a noncanonical or unexpected book. That, I think, makes the compulsion all the more interesting. I have a friend who can sometimes be seen at a bus stop or in a café dipping back into *Black Lamb and Grey Falcon* by Rebecca West. That book is ostensibly a travelogue about a trip through Yugoslavia, but as Geoff Dyer has noted, it really has two subjects: Yugoslavia and everything else. I feel much the same way about Henry David Thoreau's first and almost completely ignored, if not forgotten, book. As with *Black Lamb and Grey Falcon*, *A Week on the Concord and Merrimack Rivers* is ostensibly about, well, a week spent rowing on the two rivers designated in the book's prosaic title. But it is also about whatever else was on Thoreau's mind at the time, things that have absolutely nothing to do with river travel. Which is what makes *A Week* at once such a fascinating and, to many, a maddening book. It is an unclassifiable text and a precursor, I believe, to later experiments, such as William Carlos Williams's *Paterson* and *Spring and Now*, Paul Metcalf's fascinating collage narratives, Guy Davenport's meta-fictive assemblages, and the genre-straddling works of W. G. Sebald. Within *A Week*, one finds standard travel writing, philosophy, theology, literary criticism, music theory, poetry (Thoreau's own and in translation), extensive quotation, natural history, human history, diatribes, and dissent. And much else. Within *A Week*, Thoreau defined an enduring book as one in which "each thought is of unusual daring." By that definition, *A Week* is an enduring book. The schools of modernism or postmodernism would have immediately recognized it as one of their own, but Thoreau's own contemporaries were slow to take it up. Though the book was generally well reviewed—critics did take exception with the author's unorthodox religious ideas—it was not well remunerated. It sold two hundred copies in four years. A rueful Thoreau remarked in his journal that of the nine hundred books he owned, he had actually written seven hundred of them—all the copies of *A Week* that hadn't sold.

The book hasn't fared much better over the last 167 years. When Edward Abbey went, as the title of an essay says, "Down the River with Henry Thoreau," he took with him not Thoreau's river book—but *Walden*! Even a few years ago, Robert Sullivan, in *The Thoreau You Don't Know,* made the sweeping proclamation that *A Week* "doesn't work," that it's the kind of book "every young writer thinks he ought to write—or put together—when in fact, he probably shouldn't." Which is to say: *A Week* doesn't work in the way Sullivan wants it to, or expects it to.

I don't want to suggest that *A Week* is a better book than *Walden,* and if it weren't for *Walden, A Week* would probably have been long forgotten. But it is a more adventurous book, and there are certainly things that recommend it over Thoreau's masterpiece. You will find in it little of the captious self-righteousness that mars Thoreau's second book. Nowhere in *A Week* does Thoreau write that the rest of us lead lives of quiet desperation or have our heads filled with maggots. It doesn't contain such mean-spirited remarks, as when Thoreau claimed in *Walden* that he could do without the post office because he never received a letter worth reading (we know good and well that he treasured, at the very least, letters from Lidia Emerson, who he probably secretly loved in the way Nietzsche loved Richard Wagner's wife, Cosima). *A Week* is a more buoyant, less melancholy book than *Walden,* and it is certainly a less solipsistic book. Whereas *Walden* is all about the first person singular—as it has to be—the word *I* appears only a handful of times in *A Week*. There is only *we*: two brothers out for an adventure.

What's more, *A Week* is a book with a secret—a secret about a girl.

With his beguiling song, Orpheus lured the Dodonian oaks from the mountains of northern Greece, down to the shores of Thrace. Under Athena's priapic eye, Jason of Iolcus cut from those trees the keel and crossbeams for the *Argo,* the ship that would carry him and the Argonauts on the first great voyage of Western literature. There was, presumably, no goddess to guide Henry and John Thoreau in the construction of their more modest vessel. During the spring of 1839, the brothers built a fifteen-foot fisherman's dory behind their parents' house in Concord and christened it the *Musketaquid,* after the Indian name for their native river, a name that meant "grass-ground" or "meadow-river." White settlers renamed the river after its first plantation, but Henry Thoreau was as suspect as the natives that men could own what they did not create, and so he preferred the river's earlier, descriptive appellation. They completed construction in a week, outfitting the *Musketaquid* with a mast, two rowing stations, and detachable wheels to portage the heavy craft around the numerous falls on the Merrimack (they ended up not needing the wheels). They loaded down the boat with melons and potatoes, planning to catch or shoot whatever meat they ate during the trip. At their nightly encampments, the cotton sail would double as a tent, the mast as a tent pole.

"If rightly made," Thoreau wrote in a beautiful passage from the "Saturday" chapter of *A Week,* "a boat would be a sort of amphibious animal, a creature of two elements, related by one half its structure to some swift and shapely fish, and by the other to some strong-winged and graceful bird. The fish shows where there should be the greatest breadth of beam and depth of the hold; its fins direct where to set the oars, and the tail gives some hint for the form and position of the rudder. The bird shows how to rig and trim the sails, and what form to give to the prow that it may balance the boat, and divide the air and water best." Writer and sailor Stan Grayson has speculated that this is precisely why the brothers' dory was so narrow, and therefore tippy across the beam: it "derived from Thoreau's observation of the Concord River pickerel!"

I myself took up amateur boatbuilding when I was twice the age at which Thoreau built his first boat. That is to say, I was a thirty-two-year-old community college English teacher. I taught six classes a semester of mostly freshman comp. It kept me mentally exhausted and yearning to somehow get outside of my head, and outside of my students' heads. I needed to do something with my hands. So I signed up for a night school woodworking class in which an eight-fingered shop teacher (he lost the others to a table saw, which provided a powerful cautionary tale about, well, caution) led us each through the process of building a handsome Shaker side table. After that, I bought some basic tools: a hand plane, a circular saw, a rotary sander, a drill. My stepfather, thrilled that I had finally taken up a hobby that seemed appropriately masculine, bought me a portable workbench and a router for Christmas.

Each December, the WoodenBoat School of Brooklin, Maine, releases its slick catalog of the next year's courses. I spent hours that Christmas contemplating photos of the beautiful canoes, sailboats, and skiffs that the students would build. I finally decided to sign up for an introductory class taught by a retired lobsterman named John Karbott. We would attempt a dory similar to the Thoreaus' and learn the fundamentals of traditional clinker boatbuilding in the process. Our class met in a converted barn overlooking Naskeag Harbor. Our first lesson was, "Never be that person who leaves the coffeepot empty." Maine boatbuilders, I would quickly learn, are very serious about their coffee. Later, when John said, "Let's go over to the drooring baud and tock about scoffing," a local nurse in the class whispered to me, "Maine lobstermen don't lose their *Rs*; they just misplace them." We were going over to the *drawing* board to talk about *scarfing,* a technique for joining together sheets of plywood to give the needed length for a boat's side planks. After that, we moved on to lofting, a technique for mathematically figuring out where each plank will hit its frame as it bends into place. For someone who held down a D in high school algebra, this was rocket science, and it didn't help when a high school senior in the class turned to me and said, "You know, this is really just poor man's calculus." Still, it was thrilling to watch all those calculations actually rise into the third dimension and take shape in the sinuous lines of our dory. John Karbott insisted that we do everything in the manner of the original Massachusetts dory builders. That meant securing all the strakes with steel rivets. After a day of hammering rivets, I approached John with throbbing hands and asked if there was an easier way. "Oh yeah," he said, "you just use epoxy. Makes a much lighter boat too."

On the last day of class, all the students were treated to a lobster feast down by the harbor. Bobbing out at one of the moorings was a sleek white dory that looked uncommonly handsome to me in the late light. Its sides weren't planked but rather cut from one long piece of scarfed plywood. Yet I couldn't quit looking at its sweeping lines and elegantly tapered "tombstone" transom. When John Karbott approached me carrying a plate of empty lobster shells, he told me that this type of dory was called the Gloucester Gull. I asked if he thought I had, over the last week, developed the skills to build it. He said there was a strong possibility.

When I returned to Kentucky, I straight away ordered plans for the boat, along with *How to Build the Gloucester Light Dory* by Harold "Dynamite" Payson. This slim volume is probably the only other book I have read with the attention and determination that I devoted to *A Week on the Concord and Merrimack Rivers.* A dory is a flat-bottomed boat with no keel, thus the dories built in the late 1800s in boat shops all along the Merrimack River could be easily stacked together on large trawlers heading out to sea. The Gloucester light dory, or Gloucester Gull, is a descendant of those early scows and was conceived by a contemporary Gloucester designer, Phil Bolger. So it is also a distant relation to the Thoreau brothers' boat. Originally I aspired to build a replica of the *Musketaquid*. But I knew I didn't have the lofting skills to both design and build it based on Thoreau's brief description. So I turned instead to Bolger, who has secured a reputation and a devoted following by designing boats that anyone with marginal carpentry skills and more-than-marginal perseverance can lift off the drawing board and onto station molds. The genius of the Maine boatbuilder Dynamite Payson was to translate Bolger's concepts into clean, clear (often comic) prose. The inscription in my copy of *How to Build the Gloucester Light Dory* reads: "For Erik. Just do it! H. H. 'Dynamite' Payson."

It took me the better part of a weekend to figure out how to convert the plans' scale notation using an architect's rule; I simply don't have that kind of mind. Which is why I had to read Dynamite's book over and over, sentence by sentence. I had to translate language into math and math into wood. I don't think I ever weighed words so carefully in my life. I had never tried so hard, as we used to say back in grad school, to match the signifier with the signified. But theories of deconstruction and the arbitrariness of language are really of no use to a boatbuilder. If I didn't make the words match their meaning, I was never going to wind up with anything resembling a seaworthy vessel.

What I did have going for me was what had become a borderline obsession with the elemental beauty of the small wooden boat. Its lines were like a poem, something perfectly balanced and purified of the superfluous. It was easy to translate my enthusiasm for that quintessential form into sheer doggedness to build the Gloucester Gull. I see it now as I look back at photos of my younger, thinner self sweating in the heat of my small garage all day long in the summer of 1999.

Per Dynamite Payson's instructions, I built my boat upside down, around a set of molds, like a traditional flatiron skiff. I cut the stem and the transom from cherry and fastened them first to the fore and aft forms. Then I connected them with the long, unwieldy sides cut from marine plywood. After that I had to install chines, long pieces of oak, cut at an angle to hold the hull to the sides—to hold the whole thing together essentially. John Karbott had warned me that this would be the toughest part. Hardwood, particularly oak, doesn't naturally want to bend into such a curve, and I had no setup for steaming the wood. Instead I had to apply C-clamps at one-foot intervals and gradually tighten them around the recalcitrant chines over a series of days. Once the chines had finally succumbed to my will, it was easy enough to lay a one-inch-thick piece of plywood over the whole assembly and trace out the hull. With anchorfast nails, I attached it and the sides to the chines. I stretched a long piece of fiberglass cloth over the entire hull, painted it down with resin, and the boat was watertight. I sprung her from the molds, turned her over onto a set of sawhorses, then cut the thwarts, oar-locks, and breast hook on a band saw. Attaching the gunwales was like installing the chines in reverse, but easier since they ran along the outside of the boat. Finally I cut what's called a sculling notch into the top of the transom, one of Phil Bolger's most elegant little details. Thoreau had written that a fish's fins show the boatbuilder where to set the oars, and indeed I've watched Maine lobsterman skim from one trap to another by expertly torqueing that single oar through a sculling notch as if it were a fish's caudal fin.

My boat was finished. My next-door neighbor, an eighty-year-old undertaker, brought over a bottle of champagne. I set the champagne on the breast hook and took a picture of the long, lithe dory. Dyna-mite Payson says he can crank out a Gloucester Gull in three days. It took me the better part of that summer. With some friends, I took the boat and the bottle of champagne to the Kentucky River, where I christened her the *Ellen Sewall*.

That fall, I started a teaching job at the University of Kentucky. On the first day of class, I found myself in the elevator with the poet Nikki Finney. When she asked what I did over the summer, I said I built a wooden boat. "Ah," she said, "that's what I see in your eyes."

It makes sense that Athena helped Jason build the *Argo*; she was, after all, the Greeks' patron goddess of arts and crafts. But as that ne-glected goddess faded from our consciousness, so to a large degree has our appreciation of craftsmanship. In 1889, twenty-eight years after Thoreau died, Andrew Carnegie argued in *The Gospel of Wealth* that while preindustrial societies may have exhibited more "social equality," industrial capitalism must inevitably replace such artisan economies because mass production brings down the cost of goods and makes more of them more cheaply available. That's obviously true enough, but mass production soon proved too successful. It quickly surrounded us with the homogenous and the uninspired, and because it was cheap and ready-made, there was a lot more of it. Ugliness and blandness started to clutter our American lives. By 1925 the German poet Rilke was already complaining bitterly: "Now there are intruding, from America, empty indifferent things, sham things, *dummies of life*." And he was right, of course: most of what gets mass produced is rather sterile and lifeless, made by a machine instead of human hands. By building a wooden boat, I wanted to mount a tiny rebellion against all that bland homogeneity and make my own implied argument for the value of artisanship, craftsmanship. This was only a hobby of course, but in a wonderful little essay called "A Man's Leisure Time," Aldo Leopold wrote that a hobby is an act of defiance against the contemporary: "A good hobby, in these times, is one that entails either making something or making the tools to make it with, and then using it to accomplish some needless thing." I certainly didn't *need* a wooden boat; I'm not a Maine lobsterman after all. What's more, my boat is, as Carnegie and Ford would say, very inefficient. By the assembly line standard, it took far too much time to build, and since wood is a very permeable material, I am constantly having to repair rot and reapply paint and varnish. Also, in building my dory, I made mistakes, a lot of them. The boat is handmade, and it *looks* handmade. But that, I would like to think, is part of its charm. It's the reason men (it's always men) approach me at landings or in parking lots if I have the boat trailered. They want to see this anomaly, and they want to hear about how it came into being. The boat also represents, I think, something in their deep collective male conscience: it represents a time when men *did* build things, manly things, by hand. There is perhaps nothing more collectively masculine than a wooden boat; it's the reason you always see them in erectile dysfunction ads. The boat represents an earlier, more virile form of masculinity. As Thoreau would say, it represents a bygone era of wildness, of adventure, of getting the hell away from all things domestic. That wasn't exactly my agenda, but I can say that building the *Ellen Sewall* was one of the most satisfying things I've ever done.

Now I'm rowing between cliffs of 450-million-year-old sedimentary rock—the oldest in the state of Kentucky—that rise hundreds of feet above this river. *Rise,* however, is exactly the wrong word—the human perspective of someone floating here at the base of all that calcified rock. These spectacular cliffs didn't rise; rather, over the last five million years, the river cut this gorge across this upheaval of limestone, then wrote its autobiography on these walls. It's as if I'm drifting along the bottom of time. And while the river always writes in the present tense, the rocks reveal an always more ancient fossil history, a story of gastropods and cephalopods and trilobites. Presumably, given enough time, this river would eventually reach down to reveal the common ancestor from which we all derive our mitochondrial DNA. That would have been a moment of great rejoicing for Thoreau, who at the time he wrote *A Week* was in the process of rejecting Louis Agassiz's theory of special creation for Charles Darwin's theory of evolution through natural selection. It never bothered Thoreau that the Creator did not start out with a grand, fixed plan. He was more impressed by the way nature "perfected herself by an eternity of practice."

This morning, however, my home state shelled out more than $18 million in tax incentives to Answers in Genesis, a group of creationists who want to build in northern Kentucky a Noah's Ark theme park as a vehicle for spreading their antievolutionary views (establishment clause of the Constitution be damned). Recently the creationists began cutting down the summer habitat of the endangered Indiana bat to make way for their five-hundred-foot-long replica of the ark into which Noah, so the story goes, *saved* the Indiana bat from annihilation lo those many millennia ago. Thoreau, who had a keen sense of irony, would have loved that detail.

I suspect one of the things about *A Week* that puts readers off initially is the long section of "Saturday" that Thoreau devotes to cataloging every species of fish in the Concord River. By dividing *A Week* into seven chapters, named for the seven days of the week, Thoreau was telling his own creation story. In that story, he reenacted Adam's task of naming the animals: the perch, the dace, the pout, the pickerel, the eel, the shad, the bream that "shimmered in the water like newly minted coins." And in Thoreau's creation story, the fish had to come first because "the fish principle in nature," as he put it, was also the first principle in nature. (The first true fish actually appeared during the Ordovician era, when these limestone cliffs were also forming.) Wherever one found a body of water, fish soon appeared, Thoreau observed. It seemed like a kind of miracle, one grounded not in scripture but in the theories of evolution. The fish principle was Thoreau's own early attempt at finding a common ancestor, and he was at least on the right path. What's more, by tracing the Merrimack River to its source in the White Mountains, Thoreau was telling a very different creation story than the one handed down by the church he refused to attend. He was, in effect, running the film backward—reversing the fall.

SUNDAY

BY ALL ACCOUNTS, John and Henry Thoreau were best friends. It was John who first led Henry, two years younger, roaming through the Concord woods and later made for him a catalog of all its native birds. But the brothers were also tuned in very different keys. John was easygoing, charming, at home in a crowd. Henry was aloof, tight-lipped, awkward among strangers. His humor wasn't gentle like John's, but cutting and ironic. Henry was bookish and exacting; John wore his learning lightly. It was Henry who had a Harvard education, but it was John who was said to have a future. In August 1839, the Thoreau brothers had just finished their first year of teaching at a school for boys they started in Concord, a school prized for what educators today call experiential learning. In general, the students preferred the warmer John to the more exacting Henry. One of their best pupils was an eleven-year-old named Edmund Sewall, whose aunt, Prudence Ward, boarded with the Thoreau family. That summer, when school was out, Edmund's older sister, Ellen, came to visit her aunt and brother. John escorted the seventeen-year-old girl on walks around Walden Pond. Henry, not to be outdone, took her rowing there in the wooden boat he had built at age sixteen. At her request, he also took her berrying and to see a touring giraffe.

The only thing Ellen Sewall could not persuade Thoreau to do was go with her to church. A month before John and Henry embarked on their river trip, Ellen Sewall returned home to Scituate, on the Massachusetts coast. She described in a letter how she had cried all the way to Lexington, so sorry was she to be leaving the Thoreaus. By August, when John and Henry shoved off for their trip up the Merrimack River, they had both fallen in love with Ellen Sewall, a fact they didn't dare admit even to each other.

That first night on the river, after rowing seven miles, the Thoreau brothers set up camp on a small island near Billerica. When they awoke Sunday morning, the "auroral rosy" light suggested to Henry that this particular morning predated the fall of man, yet it still preserved what he called a "heathenish integrity." Later that morning, when some churchgoers observed the Thoreaus not observing the Sabbath, they "indulged in some heathenish comparisons," or so it seemed to Henry. That disparaging glance sets off the longest disputation about Christianity in all of Thoreau's writing, which is saying something given that much of his work contains a running debate with mainline American religion. Thoreau's views bear a striking resemblance to those of his near contemporary Friedrich Nietzsche, a man whose solitary life greatly resembled Thoreau's. (Nietzsche had a copy of Emerson's essays in his coat pocket the morning he went insane trying to defend a horse from being flogged.) Both writers believed that the Christianity practiced by the churches of their day had replaced the Gospels' radical social message with what Thoreau called "authority and respectability." That authority robbed individuals of a truly meaningful experience of the divine, something Thoreau thought existed largely beyond the realm of language and rational understanding. Men, like rivers, are born of high, hidden sources, he said. As for the language and doctrine of the church, Thoreau chided his townspeople, "You did not invent it; it was imposed upon you." For a believer in Emersonian self-reliance, this was the greatest abdication of one's own interior life. What's more, churchmen and -women had become distracted by the gospellers' and the apostles' commentaries on Christ's life rather than focusing on the life itself. Thoreau went so far as to claim that one could *only* appreciate the life of Christ by standing outside Christianity. From that perspective, a truly radical vision would appear. Here, after all, was an itinerate street preacher calling on us to abandon our wealth and our families if we hoped to find the kingdom of God, and to find our own souls by losing the world. These messages were so discomforting to Thoreau's townspeople that he simply concluded that they did not ever *read* their Bibles. "Let but one of those sentences be rightly read, from any pulpit in the land," he wrote ("Lay not up for yourselves treasures on earth," for instance), "and there would not be left one stone of that meeting-house upon another."

For all the praise Thoreau lavished on the Eastern sages he so revered, Christianity did have one thing over the contemplative religions of India and China: it was an *active* religion—men and women were called to do something, to right wrongs. The problem was they seldom did. Christianity, for them, was little more than a guarantee of life everlasting through the blood sacrifice of one man. In his typical gnomic fashion, Thoreau wrote this of the New Testament in the "Sunday" chapter of *A Week:* "I have not yet got to the crucifixion, I have read it over so many times." Like Thomas Jefferson, who excised the crucifixion from the personal Bible he created with a pair of scissors, Thoreau believed the words and deeds of Jesus were the crux of Christianity, not the death of its founder and the later interpretations of that death.

Thoreau was devising for himself what I would call a pragmatic pantheism. Like William James, he believed that a belief held significance only if it led to some significant act. Religion, said James, should be a "habit of action." Don't just be good, Thoreau wrote in *A*

Week, be good *for* something. As for his pantheism, which so upset the reviewers of *A Week,* Thoreau claimed that a man like himself, who spent so much time in the woods, did not make a good subject of Christianity, nor did the god Jehovah seem particularly interested in such a man. Rather it was the Greek gods who could much more often be found cavorting in nature, causing Thoreau to lay down this heresy: "In my Pantheon, Pan still reigns in his pristine glory, with his ruddy face, his flowing beard, and his shaggy body, his pipe and his crook, his nymph Echo, and his chosen daughter Iambe; for the great god Pan is not dead, as was rumored." This disheveled, flute-playing god looked pretty much like Thoreau himself, though Pan had much better luck with women.

But the ultimate reason Thoreau, like Nietzsche, had to reject Christianity was because it "only hopes. It has hung its harp on the willows, and cannot sing a song in a strange land." Unlike Buddhism, the Judeo-Christian religions were still lost in exile, in a sense of estrangement from this world. On that Sunday morning in 1839, Thoreau marveled at how beautiful the water willows, *Salix purshiana,* looked reflected in the mirror that the high tide had brought to their branches. These were not the trees of exile, *Salix babylonica*—Thoreau alluded to Psalms 137 three times in "Sunday"—but rather immanent symbols of the Persian garden paradise. They affirmed Thoreau's belief that he and John were floating through the original Sabbath morning.

To reject the biblical story of diaspora meant, for Thoreau, to reject a historical sense of time. To dwell in that past, in those ancient scriptures, was to remain in a kind of psychic exile. Instead Thoreau claimed, "God himself culminates in the present moment . . . and we are enabled to apprehend at all what is sublime and noble only by the perpetual drenching of the reality that surrounds us." Thoreau called that reality the poem of creation, and he said it continued uninterrupted into his own present. That poem was not a song of exile, and the Concord and Merrimack were not the rivers of Babylon. Instead, when John and Henry watched two skilled sailors glide past them in their own skiff, "It reminded us how much fairer and nobler all the actions of man might be, and that our life in its whole economy might be as beautiful as the fairest works of art or nature." That was the highest compliment Thoreau could pay a man, and it was what he aspired to in his own life. This is precisely what Nietzsche so loved about the Greek gods: they justified life by *living it themselves*—"the only satisfying theodicy!" Likewise for Thoreau, to raise one's actions, one's life, to a level worthy of contemplation—that was the finest philosophy of all, an intense ontology that needs no attendant morality or piety.

The limestone cliffs that make up the Palisades of the Kentucky River vary greatly in tone and texture. The whitest portions are referred to locally as Kentucky marble, and the indefatigable Shakers quarried that rock to build Pleasant Hill, their millennial paradise up on a tableland overlooking the river visitors can still find the Ordovician cephalopod embedded in the stone pavers of the West Family House). But those white stretches quickly turn gray or black and look as if chimney smoke has marred the stone's pristine nature. Indeed, the Palisades' sheer walls can quickly give way to freestanding columns called chimney rocks or candlesticks. In other places, the limestone becomes honeycombed with pittings, or whole caves and clefts form in the cliffs fifty feet above the river. In other places, it looks as if huge boulders have been tenuously stacked by some early god, back when rivers had gods and we took great efforts to propitiate them.

In *Four Quartets*, T. S. Eliot suggested that rivers *are* gods—fractious, unpredictable gods—who have of late gone unhonored "by worshippers of the machine." We see the river only as a problem, something to be conquered by bridges or, in the case of the Kentucky and Merrimack Rivers, by locks and dams. In the 1840s, the state of Kentucky got swept up in this country's enthusiasm for canals and the increased profits they were sure to bring. The Army Corps of Engineers eventually built fourteen locks and dams across the Kentucky River, but it proved to be no Erie Canal as far as commerce was concerned. The coal and timber barons preferred the incipient railroads, and they still do. All the dams did was turn a churning river into a series of lakes, which is where I'm floating right now. Even pleasure boating never really caught on, and so the corps eventually let the locks fall into disrepair.

Like any good environmentalist, Thoreau found the very idea of a dam offensive and unnatural. When he and John reached the dam at Billerica, Thoreau grieved that it had stymied the migration of shad to their ancient spawning pools: "Poor shad! Where is thy redress? When Nature gave thee instinct, gave she thee the heart to bear thy fate?" He even hinted darkly that one morning the town of Billerica would wake to find that a crowbar had opened the floodgates to the running fish. In the meantime, Thoreau counseled the shad to pass their summers elsewhere until the forces of nature overwhelmed the flickering fantasy that men call progress.

As the brothers were nearing the mouth of the Concord River, Thoreau wrote obliquely, "On this same stream a maiden once sailed in my boat, thus attended by invisible guardians, and as she sat in the prow there was nothing between the steerman and the sky." The maiden was Ellen Sewall, and Thoreau's love for her had, as love will, made him one with the stars. But she had slipped through his net—a story I'll get to—and so, as he lay alone at night, "the very stars seem but this maiden's emissaries and reporters of her progress." That doleful sentiment is followed by a poem of lost love in which Thoreau stoically wrote, "Still will I strive to be/As if thou wert with me." After losing Ellen Sewall, Thoreau decided that nature would have to be his bride. He moved to Walden Pond, where he wrote *A Week on the Concord and Merrimack Rivers* and where, as his poem concluded,

> *I'll walk with gentle pace,*
> *And choose the smoothest place,*
> *And careful dip the oar,*
> *And shun the winding shore,*
> *And gently steer my boat,*
> *Where water-lilies float,*
> *And cardinal flowers,*
> *Stand in their sylvan bowers.*

A few years ago I moved to the country, harboring many of the urban disaffections that drove Thoreau out to Walden Pond. But I was lucky enough to convince the woman I loved to come with me. We were married beside a creek, on a slab of limestone not far from where we float together today on the Kentucky. Of my days on the river, today is the only one on which I, like Thoreau, have a companion in my boat. Perhaps because of John's presence, *A Week* is a more sanguine book than *Walden*. And perhaps that's why I, who have now chosen companionship over solitude, prefer it. My wife, Melissa, and I each occupy a stem and stern seat in the boat I've christened the *Ellen Sewall*. A green heron dips across the river in front of us, and I say, "There goes a green heron."

Melissa looks briefly up from her book and says, "It's smaller than the blue one."

"And you don't see nearly as many of them," I add.

"Good," she said, "you can put that in your essay."

As is our usual custom during our Sundays in the boat, Melissa reads literary fiction while I write or read nonfiction. Melissa does not aspire to write; nor does she particularly aspire to read the kind of books I write. But we both love the boat and the river, and we share what the very Thoreauvian homesteader and landscape artist Harlan Hubbard once called "a communicative silence." Hubbard was speaking about his wife, Anna, with whom he shared a completely self-sufficient life for thirty-four years, first on a shanty boat floating down the Mississippi River, then in the house Harlan built for them on the banks of the Ohio River, about an hour's drive from here. Together, until Anna's death in 1986, the Hubbards lived almost completely off the land and the sun. They cultivated a garden and raised goats for food and milk, baited a trotline every evening for catfish, cut firewood for the stone hearth that Hubbard had set by hand. They were rebelling against the twentieth century in the same way Thoreau was reacting to the nineteenth. "Against what I thought wrong and false, I have been conducting a one-man revolution," wrote Hubbard. Except it was a one-man and one-*woman* revolution. The Hubbards' extraordinary marriage gives us some glimpse of what that life might have looked like for Thoreau if Ellen Sewall had joined him at Walden Pond. As for Melissa and me, while we raise a garden and some chickens, and cut our own firewood for heat, we haven't nearly achieved the Hubbards' level of rural independence; however, I do like to think that, here in the boat, we have at least achieved that happy state of being quiet together—a communicative silence.

When I put down my notebook, I pick up *A Week*. The "Sunday" chapter ends with a treatise of sorts on reading. Books are the society we keep, wrote Thoreau, and therefore we must choose them carefully. For the unchurched men and women like Thoreau, and like Melissa and me, reading can rise to a form of worship. If we read alright, said Thoreau, we would read only poetry. It is the most "natural fruit," the greatest flowering of the human mind. Novels, he maintained, should be avoided because "they have so little real life and thought in them." I've actually been swayed by that view for much of my adult life, and my library, at least before it merged with

Melissa's, consisted mostly of nonfiction and poetry. Now my Thoreau and my Mary Oliver sit beside Melissa's George Eliot and Alice Munro. And honestly, it's probably time that I temper my antinovel stance, especially given a recent study showing that people who read literary fiction possess greater levels of empathy than those who don't (one of the test cases involved reading fiction by my neighbor down the river, Wendell Berry, a man who writes beautifully in all three genres). Yet I think an important distinction still exists: The Andre Dubus III novella that Melissa is reading right now, and that I'm sure is as good as she says, *removes* her from this boat and this river, while reading *A Week* here brings the river and its inhabitants *closer*. I don't mean that it's a *better* reading experience, only that it performs a different mental function. Both reading experiences are obviously about beauty on some level, the beauty of language well rendered, but Thoreau's aim and his success was to return his reader more intensely to the natural world of the kingfishers and the riverbanks, to return the reader more intensely to his or her own life in that world. To read a book like *A Week* on a river is to, in many ways, dissolve the boundary that is the edge of the page. The kingfisher on the page and the kingfisher careening around me each make the other appear with more clarity, more *presence*. It's a kind of two-way alchemy, a transformative way of reading. For Thoreau, art was a directive, a threshold back into a more fully realized way of being in the world. The words on the page point to what Thoreau called the original scripture of the natural world. In that landscape we find the poem that writes itself: an endless improvisation. The artist should intuit the laws of that Logos so they manifest in his own work. And really, *A Week* is that kind of improvisation. It follows the river's logic, the bittern's inscrutability, the hidden mechanisms of the water lily. The world was the first and final work of art; thus he usually capitalized the word *Nature*. Nature is at once the creator and the creation, and so the one can only be seen in the other. For Thoreau, art was the way back to that world, the path out of our self-imposed exile. We do not have to hang our harps from the willows of Babylon.

As the sun began to set that Sunday in 1839, the Thoreau brothers spotted "a dark and monstrous" fish bobbing near their boat, and they suddenly remembered why the Merrimack was also called the Sturgeon River. One brother—Thoreau didn't say which—raised his rifle and delivered a charge into the "halibut-skinned monster." Which turned out to a buoy. With "each casting some blame on the other," the brothers camped at Tyngsborough and dined on potatoes instead of sturgeon.

MONDAY

MEN AND WOMEN traverse a river, Thoreau noted in the "Monday" chapter of *A Week*, "but the long-lived gods bound up or down the stream." The day before it had been the churchgoers who crossed the bridge at Chelmsford; now it was men in their work attire taking the ferry across the Merrimack (Thoreau couldn't resist comparing it to the River Styx) to chase after the business and busy-ness of the world. The brothers, for their part, would follow the path of the gods upstream, and at their leisure. I too row upstream in the early morning. Always looking for the path of least resistance, the Kentucky meanders through looping oxbows and panhandles. The inner banks are wooded or cleared for farms, while the outer banks are typically lined with walls of limestone. This morning cliff swallows dive down around my boat, where water striders—we call them Jesus bugs around here—walk on the river's surface, while trout punctuate its long sentence. In the shallows, the roots of a dead tree stick out of the water like the antlers of a young elk. Damselflies mate in midair—the male grasps the female's thorax with his terminal appendage—then they ride downstream on a raft of sycamore bark, still affixed to one another.

Today the river is quiet save the calls of a few crows. Mine seems to be the only boat on the water between locks five and six. And because of those dams, the rowing is quite easy. In places, the Palisades offer a dramatic frame of the blue sky, so that you see no more of it than you do of the green river. Thoreau wrote that he and John painted the *Musketaquid* blue and green "with reference to the two elements in which it was to spend its existence." I altered that plan slightly and painted the entire hull of my own boat blue and the inside a teal green. As such, it doesn't reflect those two elements but rather stands, or floats, in what seems to me a beautiful contrast: the blue prow cutting through the green river, and the green interior drinking in the blue sky above.

I come to one of several places where tributaries have carved wide breaks into the cliffs. The midsummer trickle of water follows a series of falls and platforms, then plunges into a small pool, where the stream has deposited a small island of scree. The force of water over time is hard to fathom and hard to overestimate. Thoreau sensed this too as he and John made their way upstream. When they reached a falls where whirlpools of water caused stones to spin in a gyrating motion for centuries, like an inverse potter's wheel slowly cutting rather precise bowls into the limestone, Thoreau proclaimed, "The finest workers in stone are not copper or steel tools, but the gentle touches of air and water working at their leisure with a liberal allowance of time." Water is indeed the most elemental sculptor. That, I think, is why the work of Constantin Brancusi appears at once so modern and so archaic. His highly burnished *Bird in Flight* looks like it was never touched by human hands. It also looks more like Thoreau's "first fish" on its evolutionary way to becoming a bird, or like the *Musketaquid,* a bird and a fish at once.

The quality of timelessness in that sculpture resides also in the limestone all around me. These obdurate, seemingly eternal walls of stone were actually formed when, half a billion years ago, the forces of water pressed together the calcium carbonate shells of primordial marine organisms. It's an idea and an expanse of time that my mind at once repels and finds utterly compelling. Throughout *A Week,* Thoreau gravitated to such natural history even as he disparaged monuments of human history, like the cemetery he and John came upon at Dunstable. It was filled with casualties of the Massachusetts Indian wars, but Thoreau remained unimpressed. "Why these stones, so upright and emphatic, like exclamation-points?" he asked. "What was there so remarkable that lived?" The birch and maple that lined the river were the real hieroglyphs to be deciphered: they told the history of the *present.* Is this landscape and this moment so uninspiring that we have to sail to Egypt to look at the pyramids, Thoreau asked? Cannot a man be the hero of his own life? Thoreau's hero, his artist of life, transforms time so that the present is always "*the heroic age itself,* though we know it not, for the hero is commonly the simplest and obscurest of men." The task of the visionary was not to foretell the future but to prophesy [per MW] the present. Thoreau was, of course, speaking about himself, an obscure young man who would indeed become famous for transcribing and transforming through art his seemingly quotidian life.

To live in the present and live by what he would later call "the gospel according to the moment," was a concept central to the Eastern religions Thoreau was absorbing in the late 1830s. "Monday" offers a long meditation on *The Laws of Menu,* a composite of Hindu scripture said to be composed by the son of Brahma. Thoreau claimed that *The Laws of Menu* could be held up to the sky as a test of its validity, its universality, its timelessness. Its sentences were like hidden lakes that reflected "our own sky in their bosom." Such were the kinds of sentences Thoreau aspired to write, ones that reflected both an inner and an outer landscape. But in "Monday," Thoreau deployed the texts of "ruminant nations" to critique what he saw as a growing number of shallow New England idealists. "It is a great pleasure to escape sometimes from the restless class of Reformers," he wrote. Sounding almost like a mouthpiece for his mentor Emerson, which many accused him of being, Thoreau argued that we must reform *ourselves* inwardly before any true outer reform can take place: "You must be calm before you can utter oracles." That meditative calmness was something Americans needed to learn from the East. Every man and woman already possessed within them the secrets of the Vedas, which could be tapped only by serene contemplation. Then conscience would steer us rightly. That conscience was a river that flowed through one's life, always fresh and trustworthy. But instead, wrote Thoreau, his contemporaries had fallen under the sway of dead institutions and the "grave of custom." They couldn't think for themselves, and so they couldn't think in a way that was true to what Emerson called "the aboriginal Self."

In "Monday," Thoreau famously wrote, "Give me a sentence which no intelligence can understand." That sentence later appeared in *Walden,* and it has puzzled readers ever since. It reads: "I long ago lost a hound, a bay horse, and a turtledove, and am still on their trail." The key to unlocking the sentence, however, lies back in *A Week,* where Thoreau quoted the Chinese philosopher Mencius, who wrote: "If one loses a fowl or a dog, he knows well how to seek them again; if one loses the sentiments of his heart, he does not know how to seek them again. The duties of practical philosophy consist only in seeking after the sentiments of the heart which we have lost; that is all." Thoreau's turtledove and house could be found again, Mencius is saying. But the bay horse—the sentiments of the heart, the laws of one's own nature—that we can recover only through a contemplative philosophy.

As for Thoreau himself, he could withdraw into contemplative isolation because he did not wish to be associated with a state that held slaves or made war on Mexico. It was the same position we find in *Walden*, where Thoreau boasted that he was doing his part to abolish slavery by living apart from, morally above, the state. But in May 1854, when President Franklin Pierce ordered a Massachusetts militia to enforce the Fugitive Slave Act and return Anthony Burns to his Virginia slave owner, Thoreau's thinking changed. He wrote in his journal, "I had never respected this government, but I had foolishly thought that I might manage to live here, attending to my private affairs, and forget it." But how could he contemplate the beauty of nature when humanity was so base. That July 4, nine years after he had begun his sojourn at Walden Pond, Thoreau delivered his most sulfurous speech at a rally organized by abolitionist William Lloyd Garrison in Framingham. Thoreau asked why the people of Massachusetts would care to uphold a constitution that found it legal to force into slavery three million men and women. Under such a system, judges and justices were nothing more than inspectors who made sure an executioner's tools were in good working order. But whoever could discern truth for him- or herself—whoever knew that slavery was an abomination—did not have to wait for or follow the laws handed down by Daniel Webster and the Supreme Court. They needed rather to obey "that eternal and only just CONSTITUTION, which He, and not any Jefferson or Adams, has written into your being." They needed to actively reject a state that would send an innocent man back into slavery. "I dwelt, before, perhaps, in the illusion that my life passed somewhere only *between* heaven and hell," Thoreau told his audience at Framingham, "but now I cannot persuade myself that I do not dwell *wholly within* hell."

Back in the "Monday" chapter of *A Week*, Thoreau had already planted the seeds for such a reversal of his go-it-alone thinking when he admitted that "Christ is the prince of Reformers and Radicals" and that perhaps there had to be a balance between the quiet, contemplative East and the restless, active West. Perhaps they were necessary counterbalances: the *via contemplativa* and the *via activa*. Perhaps true action could follow from right thinking. He even made this ecumenical suggestion, surely rare at the time, that the best of all religions should be printed together in one book, one scripture. "This is a work which Time will surely edit," he wrote brightly, though the war that broke out this week in Israel and Gaza suggests that Time will need more time, and perhaps human history will never have enough of it.

On Monday night, the Thoreau brothers made their camp beside Penichook Brook. After the usual meal of roasted potatoes and sliced melon, they "talked of distant friends" for a while, then stretched out on a buffalo skin to sleep. Off in the distance they heard a drummer calling his local militia to a country muster. The music was simple enough, but Thoreau claimed to hear in it an eternal resonance, a call back to the heroic life of nature, of wildness. The drumming stirred in him something that amounted to a revelation: Suddenly "we were in season wholly. These simple sounds related us to the stars." Thoreau felt, like Rilke's Buddha, that the entire universe was somehow his flesh, his fruit. "I see, smell, taste, hear, feel that everlasting Something to which we are all allied, at once our maker, our abode, our destiny, our very Selves," effused Thoreau.

Music is the human language that veers closest to the unsayable, to what Thoreau called "the sound of the universal laws promulgated." Pythagoras, said to be a student of Orpheus, promulgated the theory that music's harmonic laws could map both the internal realm of the *psyche* and the external realm of the *kosmos* (a term Pythagoras invented). And because music has no visual form, it best conveys the preverbal intuitions of the heart. Thoreau felt all of this lying beneath the night sky on the banks of the Merrimack. He understood how music allies "what is furthest from us" to "the greatest depth within us." Music, he wrote, "is the flower of language, thought colored and curved, fluent and flexible, its crystal fountain tinged with the sun's rays, and its purling ripples reflecting the grass and the clouds." Thoreau himself had a beautiful singing voice, and if Mrs. Nathaniel Hawthorne is to be believed, he was something of a Dionysian dancer on ice skates.

But music also reminds us of our exile. "We feel a sad cheer when we hear it," Thoreau admitted, "perchance because we that hear are not one with that which is heard." This can be an existential separation from life itself as well as an emotional separation from some beloved. "One sings only what one loses," wrote the Spanish poet Antonio Machado. Probably Thoreau was thinking of his separation from Ellen Sewall, the physical distance and his uncertainty about her feeling for him. The history of the oldest lyric, the folk song, is also the history of that loss. It began with Orpheus, who sang the loss of Eurydice, then reached on through the first lyric poet, Archilochus, up to Bessie Smith and Patti Smith. But it isn't just a lover that is lost; it can be an entire sense of belonging. Music reminds us that we have sacrificed our intuition to our intelligence, the Logos to the merely logical. Music reminds us of what we have lost and what we still could be, if we found our way back to the whole language of paradise.

Through the drummer's music, Thoreau heard the voice of "that everlasting Something," which he understood in that moment to be the inner voice of "our very Selves." In such a moment, the spirit of the Self swells within like a wind that transforms the body into a nine-valved instrument through which the everlasting Something continues its endless improvisation. "The hero is the sole patron of music," Thoreau concluded. He was listening, as it were, to his own soundtrack. The hero not only hears, but is inhabited by, the music of the eternal Self. In this way, the hero fulfills Nietzsche's ultimate charge: *become who you are.*

Off in the distance, I hear Thoreau's favorite birdsong, the flute-like trill of a wood thrush.

TUESDAY

THERE'S A LIGHT fog on the river as I pull away from the landing this morning. My body is sore from yesterday cutting up a large ash tree that had succumbed to the emerald ash borer. But the rowing stretches out my limbs until they feel pliant again. Unlike canoeing, rowing calls on the whole body to move the boat along, and for that reason it feels to me like a more meditative means of propulsion. You miss things, of course, when you have your back to the bow, so I'm often interrupting the rhythm of my stroke to turn and glance behind me. Now what I see from a distance looks like a spindly dead branch poking out of the water, but it turns out to be a motionless blue heron, hoping perhaps that I'll mistake him for that very branch. He's a cousin of the bittern that impressed Thoreau as "the genius of the shore," a pre-Socratic philosopher who still believed water was the primary element.

In many places, trees characteristic of the Inner Bluegrass region of Kentucky stand like sentinels below the gray Palisades: water maple, box elder, elm, basswood, yellowwood, walnut, and the ever-present sycamore. A painter could never do justice to so many shades of green, and so we are left, as Thoreau might say, with the work of the "original artist." (The natural world, he wrote, is "an art so cunning that the artist never appears in his work.") The Shawnee once chased Daniel Boone to the edge of the rimrock above me, where he had no choice but surrender. Instead Boone dove down into the canopy of the trees, then disappeared across the river below. The Shawnee had never seen such a brazen act from a white man, and their reverence for Boone began on that day. Or so the story goes.

Small ledges jut out from the chalky limestone cliffs and eventually become island ecosystems. Nearby, a family of turkey vultures is nesting in one of the limestone cavities high up the cliff face. The adults drift back and forth high above the river, never flapping their wings like hawks but only gliding along the thermals. Farther upstream, I find tall pink phlox blooming in the shade of a steep bank, and I remember Thoreau's observation in the "Tuesday" chapter of *A Week* that the Merrimack's high banks concealed all village life and made the country appear "much more wild and primitive than to the traveler on the neighboring roads." What's more, unlike the highway, the river did no violence to nature and was thus a superior form of travel (this from the man who claimed to walk four hours a day). There's also a repose on the river, at least there is today, that one rarely finds on the road.

I've left my watch behind, and out here on this gentle water it's easy to believe in Thoreau's gospel according to the moment. Since my boat has a high prow that tends to catch the wind, I quit rowing and a let a slight breeze push me slowly downstream. I drift. Soon after Emerson encouraged Thoreau to begin keeping a journal, the twenty-one-year-old wrote this in it: "Drifting in a sultry day on the sluggish waters of the pond, I almost cease to live and begin to be." Because of the dams, I too am drifting on sluggish water, and I too am drifting in a boat I built out of wood. From where I sit I can see the many mistakes I made, but I console myself that the great Buddhist artists of China and Japan intentionally built mistakes into their work as lessons in humility. Of course my mistakes were not intentional, but the overall effect is still that of a handsome, if imperfect, boat. Drifting here inside this moment, inside this boat, confirms for me Thoreau's sentiment that there is indeed no better place to make the subtle glide from being into *Being*, from existence into that intense experience of pure, unmediated presence—an experience that has no language because it needs none.

WEDNESDAY

TODAY IS JULY 4, and rather than take the *Ellen Sewall* out on the river, I drive with Melissa to a party held at Mundy's Landing, a two-hundred-year-old tavern and inn that overlooks the Kentucky from a high eastern bank. Most of our neighbors are here, and everyone has brought a covered dish. Our host, a talented local builder who recently restored this stagecoach stop for his family, is cooking barbecue. We mill around drinking wine, sample the amazing spread, then watch an impressive fireworks display over the river. Finally we settle into our lawn chairs around a ten-foot-high campfire and spend a few hours catching up with some friends we haven't seen in a while.

Friendship is the governing theme of the "Wednesday" chapter of *A Week*, a theme much complicated by the love triangle in which John and Henry found themselves. But a reader unaware of that fact—as nearly all readers were and still are—could make little sense of this sentence inserted, with no context, into "Wednesday": "I heard that an engagement was entered into between a certain youth and a maiden, and then I heard that it was broken off, but I did not know the reason in either case."

We learn the reason, and the context, for this in Walter Harding's indispensable biography *The Days of Henry Thoreau*. When the brothers returned from their river trip, they learned from Ellen Sewall's Aunt Prudence that her parents were vacationing at Niagara Falls. Over the older woman's objections of impropriety, John immediately set out to pay Ellen a visit. Henry, meanwhile, lamented in his journal that a parcel of heaven had been annexed from his heart. Montaigne, in his essay "On Friendship," argued that brothers could never truly be great friends because they "must of necessity often jostle and hinder one another." Thoreau, as the younger brother, must have felt jostled out of the way by John's pursuit of Ellen.

At Christmas John made a second trip to Scituate, but this time Henry went along, as did Aunt Prudence. Henry played his flute for Ellen and tried to warn her off the dangers of coffee and tea. When the brothers returned to Concord, they bombarded Ellen with gifts. John sent South American opals; Henry sent love poetry:

> *Up this pleasant stream let's row*
> *For the livelong summer's day,*
> *Sprinkling foam where'er we go*
> *In wreaths as white as driven snow.*
> *Ply the oars! Away! Away!*

When Ellen wrote back, she thanked John for the precious stones. Later she realized that she had forgotten to mention Henry's poems. "I regret it exceedingly," Ellen wrote to Aunt Prudence.

Ellen again visited Concord the following summer, and the brothers again vied for her time and affections. When she returned home to Scituate, John again followed, though this time Aunt Prudence was determined to insinuate herself on the visit. But one evening when John and Ellen were walking along the coast, their chaperone stopped to rest on a rock and John seized the moment: He took a knee and asked Ellen to marry him. Startled, Ellen said yes. But by the time they returned home, she was having second thoughts. Her mother reaffirmed those doubts by assuring Ellen that her conservative, Unitarian father would never approve of his daughter marrying into a family that was friends with the transcendentalist heretic Emerson. Ellen told John that she had reconsidered her decision. He accepted the news with grace, while Henry saw it as an opening, slim though it be. Deploying the nautical metaphors he often used with writing about Ellen, Henry proposed to her in a letter that no longer exists. What does exist is a letter from Ellen's father telling her to reject Henry in terms that were "*short, explicit,* and *cold.*"

There is one final mystery, though, the one Thoreau alludes to in his oblique sentence: Why did Ellen reject John? It was Henry, after all, who was friends with Emerson, not John. And of the somewhat eccentric Thoreau family, John was the least so. Though his health was sometimes poor, he otherwise seemed like a perfectly eligible husband. No, the real reason Ellen Sewall turned down John's proposal, as she told her daughter years later, was that she loved Henry. But Ellen had been so mortified by her initial acceptance of John that she acquiesced to her father's wishes regarding Henry. Ellen never visited the Thoreaus again.

"My Friend is not of some other race or family of men," Thoreau wrote in "Wednesday," but "flesh of my flesh, bone of my bone. He is my real brother." My *real* brother. The phrase sounds almost cruel in a book about the journey of two biological brothers, brothers who had always seemed to earn from one another the capitalized *F* of Thoreau's "Friend." Certainly the slight was informed by the business over Ellen Sewall. But really, the sentence falls consistently within a darkly honest meditation on friendship.

From the start, the capital *F* suggests how Thoreau would treat friendship as some apotheosis that no actual man or woman could ever achieve. Including Thoreau himself: "I would that I were worthy to be any man's Friend." Perhaps if we put the word in lowercase, friendship would be easier to accomplish. But that is precisely Thoreau's point: he didn't aspire to be a mere friend, which he compared to honor among rogues. By contrast, the Friend praises our aspirations, not our performances. The Friend attends to the office of our spirits. The Friend acts out of impulse, not calculation. The Friend is kind to our dreams. The language of Friendship is meaning, not words. All of which is to say, Thoreau harbored a dream of Friendship in which men discourse like gods. Perhaps that is the way Thoreau hoped he and Emerson would conduct their conversations once they became Friends. But alas, wrote Thoreau in a particularly painful passage, "Our actual Friends are but distant relations of those to whom we are pledged. We never exchange more than three words with a Friend in our lives on that level to which our thoughts and feelings almost habitually rise. One goes forth prepared to say, 'Sweet Friends!' and the salutation is, 'Damn your eyes!'" We aspire to a rare and unencumbered level of intimacy, but most often we fail to reach it. Though "our fates at least are social," we are constantly failing our friends—failing to live up to their most (generous) image of us and failing to communicate with the fullness of feeling that we had hoped to bring forth. Our thoughts run to slander. "The heart is forever inexperienced," wrote Thoreau.

Perhaps because of that, Thoreau's ideal version of Friendship exists only in the actual friends' absence. "When they say farewell," he wrote, "then indeed we begin to keep them company." Then the friend becomes a Friend again, the ideal version of his or her departing self. True Friendship needs such distance, said Thoreau, because it needs to be nurtured in solitude and silence "to prepare ourselves for a loftier intimacy." Yet from inside his own solitude, it seems that Thoreau devised the perfect, impossible Friend, the one who never would appear. Perhaps because he valued his solitude so much, only such a Friend would be worthy of intruding upon it. Of course Emerson visited Thoreau almost daily at Walden, but he too became exasperated with Thoreau's intractableness and coldness. Why couldn't the man just put aside all his noble principles for an evening and gossip over a glass of wine, wondered the older transcendentalist? But Thoreau seemingly could not, and it badly strained his friendship with Emerson. "The only danger in Friendship is that it will end," wrote Thoreau. "Perhaps no one is noble or wise or charitable or heroic enough to maintain a lasting Friendship." And so, he concluded, this drama we enact almost daily "is always a tragedy."

There are, I think, many grim and difficult truths to be found in Thoreau's thoughts on friendship. By being so demanding and intransigent, he points to the countless ways we fail each other daily, even when we had hoped to do just the opposite. But he also calls attention to the possibility that we might rise to the level of a *deserving* friendship, one wholly devoid of guile, jealousy, and misunderstanding. Perhaps we might attain a level of transparency that wouldn't seem like vulnerability, at least not a vulnerability that a friend would exploit. While observing the "tragedy" of human frailty, Thoreau still held out hope that we might one day rise above it all, perhaps even *evolve* into more worthy social animals.

In the end, John blamed Ellen's absence from both brothers' lives on Henry's obtuse attempt to win Ellen for himself. A distance developed between the Thoreau brothers, one that greatly troubled Henry. But at the end of "Wednesday," he wrote that he had an ameliorating dream. It was about John, and though Henry actually had the dream much later, after their doomed proposals, he inserted it here at the end of his troubled thoughts on Friendship:

> I dreamed this night of an event which had occurred long before. It was a difference with a Friend, which had not ceased to give me pain, though I had no cause to blame myself. But in my dream ideal justice was at length done me for his suspicions, and I received that compensation which I had never obtained in my waking hours. I was unspeakably soothed and rejoiced, even after I awoke, because in dreams we never deceive ourselves, nor are deceived, and this seemed to have the authority of a final judgment.

THURSDAY

THE THOREAU BROTHERS' Thursday actually took a week, though Henry oddly included in *A Week* none of what happened when he and John moored the *Musketaquid* at Hooksett Falls; set out on foot for Concord, New Hampshire; and then caught a stage-coach from Concord up to the foothills of the White Mountains, where they climbed until the headwaters of the Merrimack River was but a small channel that they "crossed at a stride."

FRIDAY

THE BUCKEYE IS the first tree to leaf out here in the Inner Blue-grass region, and now, four months later, the tips of its leaves are beginning to turn umber. That, along with a cool, overcast morning, makes today feel prematurely autumnal. John and Henry felt it too as they woke on the last day of their trip. They had made it back to the *Musketaquid* the night before, and Friday morning they raised their sail for the first time. "The north wind stepped readily into the harness which we had provided, and pulled us along with good will," wrote Thoreau. With a paddle now plunged deep through their own sculling notch, their fish-fowl-boat transformed into Pegasus, so that John and Henry "felt each palpitation in the veins of our steed, and each impulse of the wings which drew us above." The trip to Hook-sett Falls had taken six days rowing upstream, but this wind would sweep them back to their native Concord by that Friday night.

In the Book of Isaiah, the prophet derided the quick papyrus skiffs that flew up and down the Nile as messenger boats. Their Ethiopian builders had dared to compete with the Maker, who in retaliation would one day raze their villages, leaving "nothing fashioned by their fingers." Isaiah saw man's creations as an affront to the Creator. But for Thoreau, we are never more religious than when we allow the divine law of nature to flow through the hands of the builder. When the Thoreaus came upon some carpenters mending an up-turned scow on the riverbank, "we realized that boatbuilding was as ancient and honorable an art as agriculture, and that there might be a naval as well as a pastoral life." In his lifetime, Thoreau would publish one book about the pastoral life and one about the naval.

As the brothers sailed by the farms along the Merrimack, Tho-reau mused, "How fortunate were we who did not own an acre of these shores, who had not renounced our title to the whole." Owning nothing, they owned everything. It's a sentiment similar to one expressed in the essay "Walking," where Thoreau invented an etymology of the word *saunterer*, positing that it came from the root *sainte terre*, meaning a "holy lander," a religious wanderer, a mendi-cant. Having no home, he is at home everywhere. The saunterer, he wrote, is "no more vagrant than the meandering river." Back on the meandering Merrimack, Thoreau seemed to feel this impulse even more intensely as he rode the aquatic highway no one owns.

Agriculture is the emblem of our exile, the punishment for our first disobedience. We think of Thoreau as the quintessential Amer-ican agrarian because of his bean fields at Walden Pond, but in *A Week*, he wrote that his genius "dates from an older era than the agricultural." He would rather cut a furlough with his oar than a plough. He yearned more for the wildness of the woods and rivers. Gardening was too "civil and social," and it lacked "the vigor and freedom of the forest and the outlaw." As in so many other things, Thoreau took the Indian as his model here. It wasn't the native who needed civilizing, he wrote, it was his townspeople who needed to awake from their own "slumbering intelligence." The well-tended English gardens Thoreau observed along the banks of the river were yet another symbol of an attenuated intellect, specifically a Western poetry that had shrunk into a hothouse flower. "There are other, savager, and more primeval aspects of nature than our poets have sung," he wrote. "It is only white man's poetry." Where was the poet who could step outside the narrow confines of the drawing room or the Petrarchan sonnet? Emerson voiced similar complaints in his essay "The Poet." Both men were waiting, though they didn't know it at the time, for Walt Whitman to arrive on the scene, and he did in 1855 with the first edition of *Leaves of Grass*. In *A Week*, Thoreau wrote that when reading Homer, "It is as if nature spoke." After reading *Leaves of Grass*, he wrote in his journal, "It was as if the beasts had spoken."

What about Thoreau's own poetry in *A Week*? The quality varies vastly. The freshness of both his language and his ideas often seemed to leave Thoreau when he turned to poetry. He seemed to become cramped, constricted by the form, too ready to choose easy rhyme. When he first read Walt Whitman, he must have recognized immediately in that atavistic free verse the kind of poetry he was calling for in *A Week* but could not himself create. In the end, Thoreau abandoned poetry altogether, justifying that decision with this two-line poem in the "Friday" chapter:

> *My life has been the poem I would have writ,*
> *But I could not both live and utter it.*

For Thoreau, the word must become the deed, and life itself must rise to the level of the poem. Thus began the great crescendo of *A Week*. Everything has been building toward this Zarathustrian moment in which Thoreau looked around to find that "Men nowhere, east or west, live yet a *natural* life." Men talked too much of being spiritualized when what they in truth needed to be was more naturalized to the world at hand. "Here or nowhere is our heaven," Thoreau concluded as a final punctuation to his "Sunday" thoughts on religion and the holy. His reversal of the fall was now complete. We need to pray for no higher realm than this world, this "*purely sensuous life*." The holy is all around us, though we see it not. Yet the secret to happiness was to obey nature—one's own and the one we find in the woods and rivers around us. The secret of happiness was to obey the sentiments of the heart and to live in accord with the economy of nature. "Did not he that made that which is *within,* make that which is *without* also?" asked Thoreau in a paraphrase of Luke 11:40. In the Gospel of Thomas, Jesus would state the matter even more concisely: "The kingdom of God is inside you and it is outside you." The inner landscape and the outer landscape were but reflections of the same two-sided mirror. Thoreau had lost the happiness he might have had with Ellen Sewall, but he learned that these two natures would sustain him, as he wrote to his editor Horace Greeley: "I am convinced, both by faith and experience, that to maintain one's self on this earth is not a hardship but a pastime, if we will live simply and wisely."

As I row upstream on this humid Friday afternoon, families of painted turtles, sunning themselves on deadfalls, drop reluctantly into the water when I draw close. They almost always plunge down in descending order, from largest to smallest, as if the younger ones don't quite understand what I might represent. Rowing a bit farther, I pass a snapping turtle sunning on his own dead bough. But unlike the painted turtles, this ancient and intimidating creature doesn't move, only challenges me with his unblinking, antediluvian eye. With his anvil of a head and a carapace that looks like a relic from the Trojan War, *Chelydra serpentina* is a formidable presence, and with that yellow eye, he seems to be intimating: *I've been on this river far longer than you, and I'll be here after you're gone.* I look away first, then notice that a butterfly's wings have become waterlogged in the middle of the river. Just as I reach an oar out to lend assistance, a gar with its alligator snout snatches the insect into its watery underworld. The river seems sinister today—all jaws and menace. In

A Week, Thoreau warned readers not to romanticize nature, not to declaw it with effete romantic thoughts or airy poetry. An animal's innocence wasn't measured by its beauty or benign nature in Thoreau's Eden.

But if these preternatural creatures are trying to drive me from the river, they may succeed. This might be my last day of rowing and drifting for a while. Soon I will have to turn my attention to teaching again, to devising syllabi and lectures. After their river trip, John and Henry Thoreau taught for another year at their boys' school, but then they abruptly closed the doors on April 1, 1841. John was fainting in class from violent nosebleeds and uncontrollable coughing. He had become too frail to keep teaching, and neither the children nor Henry wished to continue without him. The real problem was TB, the family curse. John set out on a tour of New Hampshire, hoping the mountain air would clear his lungs.

Then, on New Year's Day 1842, he nicked his finger shaving. A week later, his limbs began to ache. Then he developed lockjaw. A doctor was called from Boston, and he told John there was no hope. "The cup that my Father gives me, shall I not drink it?" he replied. John told his brother that he was "only going on a short journey." Three days later, he died of tetanus in Henry's arms.

After John's death, Thoreau began to imagine his manuscript for *A Week* as a pastoral elegy, and so in keeping with that poetic tradition, he never actually named John in the book. Yet we find one final symbol of the two brothers as they rowed the last stretches of their native river. They saw the silhouette of two herons flying overhead, and it seemed to Thoreau that these ancient creatures—dinosaurs, really—would not "alight in any marsh on the earth's surface, but, perchance, on the other side of our atmosphere." In the Vedas, these two birds symbolized the two selves: the mortal form and the immortal formlessness of the original self, the face we had before we were born. At the end of *A Week*, those two selves become the mortal brother and his disappearing other.

A week after John's death, Henry developed the same symptoms as John. "You may judge that we are alarmed," Emerson wrote to his brother William. But the symptoms where psychosomatic, a stoic brother's form of grieving. However, as soon as the symptoms disappeared, Emerson's five-year-old son, Waldo, died of scarlet fever. Thoreau, who had lived with the Emersons for two years as a general handyman, loved the child and had given him endless hours of avuncular attention, carving toy boats and building him birdhouses.

A month after Waldo's death, Thoreau sent to Lucy Brown, Emerson's sister-in-law, a letter that is one of our literature's most beautiful meditations on loss. "What right have I to grieve," he wrote, "who have not ceased to wonder? We feel at first as if some opportunities of kindness and sympathy were lost, but learn afterward that any *pure grief* is ample recompense for all. That is, if we are faithful; for a great grief is but sympathy with the soul that disposes events, and is as natural as the resin of Arabian trees. Only Nature has a right to grieve perpetually, for she only is innocent." Thoreau would turn to the natural world, he would turn to Walden Pond, for his solace, his recompense. There he would wonder instead of grieve for John, Ellen, and Waldo.

But from that point on, Thoreau found himself very much alone in the world. And so like Nietzsche's Zarathustra—like Nietzsche himself living alone in the Alps—Thoreau made solitude and silence his companions. *A Week* ends with a meditation on each. "As the truest society approaches always nearer to solitude, so the most excellent speech finally falls into Silence," he wrote. Due to death, departure, and his own disposition, Thoreau was approaching both. He would be the solitary plover, the single heron perched in the tree of his own wonder.

Writing rises out of that wonder, as Thoreau's beautiful first book shows, but it also descends back into it, and again into silence. It is the silence of Job after he was presented, by the voice of the whirlwind, the grandeur of the natural world. It is the silence of humility and reverence before the poem of creation, the unroofed church, the wholeness of being.

IN THE LAND OF ROCK AND SKY

W e were standing, about ten of us, at the top of Fannarakbreen Glacier, bound together by a thick rope and a common desire not to disappear under thin ice. It was the height of summer in Norway, and down below, the annual glacial melt was well under way. Our guide seemed to be issuing very comprehensive instructions in Norwegian, but his English translations—meant solely for me, the only American—were much shorter and lacked, I thought, the proper cautionary zeal. The gist of it was this: the glacier was moving slowly, like a bear turning slowly in its sleep, and could not wholly be trusted.

Clinging to another rope, knotted at one-foot intervals, we lowered ourselves down Fannaraknosi, a nearly vertical precipice of ice and snow, to reach the glacier proper. It sloped about a mile down to the timberline of Norway's Jotunheimen National Park, the troll-haunted mountains where Henrik Ibsen set his dramatic poem *Peer Gynt*. We started moving like one awkward animal across the glacier. Much of it was still covered with snow, which could obscure newly formed crevasses in the ice. As we walked parallel to a deep fissure, I could hear water rushing beneath it. Slowly, we wound our way around the soaring abutments that frame this glacier and the intensely blue pools, where the ice had grown so dense that it absorbed all other colors of the spectrum. When we finally circled down to the terminal moraine near the timberline, I asked the guide if global warming was having an effect on this particular glacier. He pointed to a boulder fifty yards away and said, "Five years ago, the ice reached over to that rock."

By Himalayan standards, I suppose Fanarakbreen Glacier isn't all that spectacular. But it *is* melting, as is nearly every other glacier in Norway, and it is another graphic indicator—not a computer model or a soaring line graph—that sea levels are rising and, for millions of people, mostly poor people, drinking water is disappearing. When I had flown into Oslo ten days earlier, I had seen out the plane's window a much larger and more ominous melting glacier—the Greenland ice sheet. Recently, NASA's leading climatologist, James Hansen, predicted that once atmospheric levels of carbon dioxide reach 350 parts per million, the melting of the Greenland ice sheet will be irreversible and sea levels will rise twenty-three feet. Hanging there in the sky above Greenland, I found myself in an oddly symbolic interval. I was halfway between my ancestral home-land of Norway and my hometown of Lexington, Kentucky—the city that, according to a recent report, contributes more to melting glaciers, per capita, than any other place in the United States.

My grandfather was a country preacher for sixty years in the Tide-water area of eastern Virginia. He used to tell me that I was named after Erik the Red, the Viking pirate who was kicked out of the Scandinavian colony on Iceland by his own people around 980 CE. After that, Red Erik packed up his family and sailed to Greenland to start a new colony. Back home in Norway, his people were busy converting from the worship of Thor and Odin to a reverence for a more peaceable Mediterranean street preacher. To do his part, Norway's King Olaf was capturing Icelandic pagans when they came to his shores and threatening them with mutilation unless they converted to Christianity. Not surprisingly, the new religion caught on, and by the end of the first millennium, Leif Eriksson, the son of Erik the Red, had introduced Christianity to his father's colony in Greenland. The Nordic marauders put down their blood axes and took up the cause of peacefulness. Today, the Nobel Peace Center sits in the heart of Oslo, Norway, just a few miles from its Viking Museum.

Because that restless family is widely thought to have been the first Europeans to reach North America by boat, a statue of Leif Eriksson now stands outside the Mariners Museum in Newport News, Virginia. When I visited my father's parents in the summer, my grandfather would take me to see the bronze Viking staring out across the horizon. And though my grandfather used to tell me I was actually a descendant of Red Erik, in truth we never traced our family lineage back beyond a Norwegian woman named Wilhelmenia Frederickson. She was my grandfather's grandmother. The population of Norway was expanding rapidly during the 1880s, and therefore the size of family farms started to shrink. Many could no longer afford to stay on the land. So Wilhelmenia Frederickson married a Swede named Will Buhler, and they immigrated to Chicago in 1888.

I suppose I've wanted to visit Norway ever since my grandfather tricked me into believing his harmless conjectures about our Viking past. And recently, the more I've found myself writing about environmental problems in the United States—particularly the mountaintop-removal strip mining that is destroying the eastern part of my home state—the more I've noticed how all the Nordic countries consistently outperform the rest of the world when it comes to issues of sustainability, alternative energy, and a form of "steady-state" economics that doesn't measure a nation's health and wealth solely by the amount of resources it consumes. Norway ranks higher than all other countries on Yale University's Environmental Sustainability Index. And as a country, it has divested completely from coal.

So when I learned that Lexington, Kentucky—due primarily to its reliance on coal—contributes more, per person, to the melting of Norway's glaciers than any other place in America, I decided it was finally time to bring the genealogical line full circle and head off to the land of Red Erik, Erik Bloodaxe, and all those other obstreperous Eriks for whom I was named.

The Norwegian word for "footpath" is *wanderwege*. It's a fun word to say out loud, even if you don't know the language: "wander-wiggy." And Norway is certainly a country of wanderers—men, women, and children who spend a great deal of time exploring their mountains, glaciers, and fjords. The footpaths that wind throughout the country's national parks are connected by thirty huts, where Norwegians bed down for the night, get dinner and breakfast, then set out for another summer day of wandering.

For a week, I had been wandering from hut to hut throughout Jotunheimen National Park, where Norway's tallest mountains tumble into each other like jagged, crashing waves. On my last full day before returning to Oslo, I had planned to climb Mount Fannaraki. At 6,775 feet, it was Norway's third-highest mountain, and clinging to the top of Fannaraki sits the country's remotest hut.

But first I had to circle from the base of the glacier to the foot of the mountain. I struck out across the rocky terrain, which had been sculpted by the ice into stark hanging valleys. The highest peaks had, for the time being, all withdrawn to the horizon, and I felt as if I were walking across the bottom of the vaulting sky, reflected like an empty mirror in the small lakes. The air grew mild with my descent, and it seemed as if all four seasons were competing to claim this day. All throughout the Jotunheimen, melting snow was creating beautiful bowls of water, still blue lakes. The *wander-wege* meandered over snowfields and across shallow streams. In some places, the snow took on a rosy, almost pink hue, created by the algae *Chlamydomonas nivalis,* which makes its home around ice crystals. The reddish pigment protects chlorophyll from exposure to sunlight at high elevations.

There was no sign here of human intervention or human artifice, except for the crudely stacked cairns that bore the trail blaze—a bright red *T.* I felt a rare, intense immediacy walking across this spare plateau. It suddenly occurred to me that I had been trying all my life to get to this place. Here, there was nothing standing between me and the natural world. Almost everything that goes by the name "culture" had dropped away. And here I was, performing the most natural of animal acts: wandering.

Back in my grandfather's Baptist church, we used to sing at Christmas the John Jacob Niles hymn "I Wonder as I Wander." What we were supposed to wonder about, as we wandered, was

> *How Jesus the Saviour did come to die*
> *For poor on'ry people like you and like I.*

But on this day, I wasn't feeling particularly ornery. I was feeling quite elated, in fact, to be striding through this glacial wilderness. No one had to save me today—I myself felt quite up to the task.

Still, John Jacob Niles was right about this—walking does often feel like the measure of thought. Perhaps Norway's most renowned walker and thinker was the philosopher Arne Naess. Born in 1912 in Bergen, Norway, Naess introduced modern mountain climbing to Norway, along with a complementary ecological and philosophical movement called deep ecology. Naess actually called deep ecology an "ecosophy," whose central tenet is to dethrone *Homo sapiens* from atop the Great Chain of Being, so that all life could be seen as having intrinsic value. Until his death in 2009, Naess called for an "ideological change" in the West whereby we replace our "high standard of living" with "appreciating life quality." That is to say, we should stop mistaking accumulation for wealth, or a certain standard of living for life itself. Naess believed that Norwegians came more naturally to this way of thinking because of a national attitude of *friluftsliv,* which roughly translates as the "free-air life." When winter breaks, Norwegians take to their mountains in a way Americans do not. What drives them there, according to Naess, is "a positive feeling for areas that are not obviously dominated by human activity." It was an easy feeling to understand, wandering through the expansive, rugged terrain of the Jotunheimen. As I drifted down into Skogadalsboen Valley, vegetation returned. I recognized, growing under the birch trees, a violet wildflower known back home as delphinium. Further down, glacial melt was turning the Ulta River into a green, churning body of water. A wooden footbridge led me across it to the base of Mount Fannaraki. There stood a wooden sign that read LUKK GRINDA. "Good luck." It wasn't exactly the sentiment I was looking for, but perhaps I was mistranslating its intent. Certainly it meant encouragement, not irony. From my short experience, Norwegians did not seem a particularly ironic people.

I started up the narrow trail, where light green ferns grew around many of the larger stones that lined the path, and often were the path, up Mount Fannaraki. The day was beautiful and clear. Small blue butterflies, spring azures, flitted among the low-growing juniper. The only trees that reach this elevation are birch, and because of climate change, they are climbing to even higher altitudes.

Occasionally I heard the dull clanking of bells, then noticed a small cluster of sheep grazing in the sparse mountain pastures that swoop down through the Jotunheimen. A stream meandered down around the rocks almost as slowly as I climbed them. I crossed over it in several places and each time paused to splash the cold water on my face. On some of the rocks near the stream, I noticed the small carcasses, or at least the remains, of what looked to be some kind of brown mouse. Jervvassbu Glacier hung glistening off in the distance.

After about two hours of climbing, I dropped my pack and settled down into the hollow of a large rock covered in lichens. I ate a few slices of salami, then leaned back and closed my eyes.

"A good soldier takes a nap whenever he can!"

Startled, I glanced up at a tan, shirtless man who looked to be in his sixties. "That's a saying we used to have in the Norwegian army," he explained cheerfully. Then he added, "You are the American from the glacier walk."

"Oh, right," I said, now understanding why he knew to speak to me in English. He wore dark sunglasses, and his short gray hair poked in all directions.

"We don't see many Americans."

"Good. I came to get away from them."

He smiled, enigmatically I thought. "Up here, you get mostly Germans and Swedes."

"What about the Danish?" I asked.

"Agh," he replied, "Danes don't know how to walk. Too much . . ." and he raised an imaginary cigarette to his lips.

I asked about the small patches of fur on the trail. He said they were the remnants of mountain mice and had probably been killed by ermine, or a smaller mammal called the least weasel. It was a good thing too; when the mouse population spikes, their feces make the streams undrinkable.

"Well, enjoy your nap," he said, waving and wandering on.

I ate a few more slices of salami and some cheese, then shouldered my rucksack. Higher up the trail, the narrow Jervvasseliv River began stampeding down around the ridge side in quick cutbacks. Above the timberline, the rivers gave way to a series of crater lakes, some hollowed out by cirque glaciers that rotate against the bedrock, others perhaps the work of dormant volcanoes. Snow was still melting at the edge of these tarns, which seemed to be turning the sky an even denser blue. The clouds now hung at the same elevation as the ridge marking the horizon.

The trail circled a larger lake, the Jervatnet, then led up to a ledge, where I was startled to find a small cabin lashed to the side of the mountain with guy wires. About fifteen by ten feet wide, the cabin sat perched on a foundation of flat stones. I couldn't resist peering through a window. Inside were two empty rooms; in one stood a neat wooden table with two chairs and a small woodstove, and the other housed a narrow bunk bed. The austere interior looked like something Van Gogh might have painted. If anything embodied the essence of philosophical solitude, surely it was this extreme yet somehow inviting abode. Who lived here? Perhaps the shepherd of the flock I had passed on my way up. But I found myself wanting to imagine that a lone philosopher sat at that table, slowly crafting some tractatus inspired by the awesome mountains that rose around him or her.

I had read that Arne Naess spent summers in his own alpine hut, farther south, in the Hallingskarvet Mountains. Standing beside this cabin, I could easily see how the deep ecology movement might have originated in such a place. At this elevation, one must indeed admit that human beings have no dominion at all over this harsh landscape. According to Naess, the fundamental lesson here is modesty. And like Mosaic Law, it is a lesson that should be carried down from the mountain and enacted in the cities, where we most often tend to become immodest in terms of what we take from nature. Of course, no one likes to be *told* to be modest—the Israelites probably weren't thrilled to see Moses hauling a stone tablet full of *shalt nots*—so it turns out to be a hard message to translate down from the mountaintop.

In cities, surrounded by all manner of human contrivances, we can more easily convince ourselves that *Homo sapiens* are the main characters in the world's drama and that if we create problems, we will also invent new ways to solve them. But at five thousand feet, where relying on the bare essentials is the name of the game, such thinking seems the product of outlandish hubris. "Only philosophies that impose sharp subject–object dualism try to trace a border between the self and 'its' geographical surroundings," Naess wrote. Yet that was precisely the project of many seventeenth-century Enlightenment thinkers—to set up a profound separation between the talking animals and the rest of the world. John Locke typified this position when he wrote that "the intrinsic natural worth of anything consists in its fitness to supply the necessities or serve the conveniences of human life."

Here in the Jotunheimen, that kind of Lockean thinking does seem unsound and immodest. Here the human ego can't help but feel real humility. From such an elevated perspective, we might cease to see the natural world, its flora and fauna, as simply a collection of objects. Rather we might begin to see the objects around us as really only other *subjects*. Then we might develop, or rediscover, a psychological faculty that seems to have gradually atrophied since Locke's time—a feeling of empathy.

One morning a few years ago, on a visit to New York, I was trying to navigate the subway when a train approached my platform. A throng of businessmen and -women rushed from it, and in that mad dash, someone's careless foot crushed the cane of a blind man standing near me. No one, including me, stopped to help him. He fell to the concrete and reached furiously around for the remnants of his shattered cane. "Do I have all the pieces?" he cried out. Nobody was listening. I stood there paralyzed. Why didn't I do something? Why didn't anybody else? Had they inoculated themselves against such daily pathos? Would I be *embarrassed,* in front of these New

Yorkers, to be seen helping this man? Would I be embarrassed by my empathy? Finally a man wearing a yarmulke stooped down to gather up the scattered sections of the blind man's cane, then helped him up the stairs into the street. And that simple act stung me with a shame I carried throughout the city for days.

I suppose that scene came back to me on Mount Fannaraki because the mountain seemed like the opposite of the New York subway. It was a solitary place where one could calmly contemplate the problems of the world below. Perhaps it was a place where a philosopher like Arne Naess could even begin to solve some of them. It was the kind of place where he had conceived the principles of the deep ecology movement and had shown how they might ultimately find relevance in the subterranean world of the crowded subway.

The American philosopher William James (who had some influence on Arne Naess) once said that mountain climbing was his "main hold on primeval sanity and health of soul." Halfway up Fannaraki, I could feel in my own mind and body what James meant. To recover that sense of belonging to a natural landscape—it did seem like the right trajectory for recovering the sanity of one's own nature. That's probably because we spent 98 percent of our evolutionary past wandering such places as small bands of nomadic omnivores. The human mind evolved and expanded *here,* not in cities. In some very deep psychological sense, the mind still feels at home in the "wilderness" that was really the domestic domain for almost all our species's existence.

From the small cabin, I could see the tiny outline of another dwelling at the top of Fannaraki. That was where I needed to end up, so I set off again. From the bottom of a long snowfield, I saw the older man from the Norwegian army, sunning on a boulder in the middle of that vast whiteness. He waved from the rock and asked if I wanted company. I said sure, and he scampered down. When

I asked his name, he said it was Victor. Then he added with pneumonic conviction, "Think Victory!"

I was indeed starting to think that I might make it victoriously to the top of Mount Fannaraki. But the steepest work was still ahead. Soon the path turned into a staircase of stones, interspersed with steep snowbanks. The only life here, besides us, was the green lichens that clung, in their marriage of algae and fungi, to the cairns marking the trail.

Up these scree slopes, Victor climbed ahead of me, steady and sure-footed. We had to shimmy through several narrow corridors of rock. The trail had now utterly disappeared. We were simply lunging from one boulder to another.

"According to the old stories," Victor said, "the gods were angry once and rained stones down on everybody's head." Well here they were, rearranged by glaciers but still presenting impressive obstacles, an object lesson to men who anger gods.

We finally reached a small plateau, where, through a crevice between two smooth slabs of rock, we could see the Jervvasseliv River gushing from its source. Lying flat on our stomachs, Victor and I reached down through the crack to fill our water bottles from this mountain stream.

Then we both leaned back to quaff our rarified draughts. After we caught our breath, Victor asked where I was from. When I said Kentucky, he paused and then replied, "Don't you have a problem there with, how do you say it, mine stripping?"

I said that we did indeed have a problem with strip mining, and I briefly explained how coal operators were blowing the tops off the Appalachian Mountains and dumping everything that wasn't coal into the streams below. Victor took a long drink of water, stared down for a moment, and then said, "That would never happen here. We would never let corporations have that much power." I nodded.

Then he added, "In Norway, we always think of our grandchildren's generation."

As I stared out at the snowcapped peaks on the horizon, I thought about my own mountains back home. Because the Appalachians are much older than the Jotunheimen, they no longer rise to these sublime heights. Though they represent the most biologically diverse ecosystem in North America, their modest size seems to make them vulnerable to attack and exploitation, in a way that the Rockies or the Sierras out west are not. And of course, unlike those mountains, or these mountains, the Appalachians are stratified with a great deal of the mineral that heats and cools the majority of American homes. Those who want to defend the Appalachian Mountains usually end up fighting against the public opinion that the country *needs* that coal and that the destruction of the Appalachians is simply inevitable.

I suppose my own frustration that defending actual American landscapes is so often seen as un-American prompted me to encourage Victor in a little more US-bashing. But he didn't take the bait.

When I expressed my admiration for Norway's lack of crime or political corruption, Victor replied, "We don't have that many people here. If we had as many people as you do in America, we'd have a lot of crazies too."

He did say, however, that when a Norwegian soldier leaves the service, the firing pin is removed from his army-issue rifle. It seemed an incredible detail, something unimaginable in the United States. Compared to Americans' general attitude about the extent to which individual rights trump larger societal concerns such as gun violence, I really was on the other side of the world.

We hoisted our packs and started climbing again. Above the headwater, the boulder paths turned mostly into deep snowfields.

There were no other tracks, no compacted path to follow. Victor and I seemed to be on a bit of a fool's errand, and as I would learn later, most hikers choose to go down, not up, this steeper, western side of Mount Fannaraki.

My shoulders were baking in the sun, but my legs and feet were freezing. Certainly, I told myself, the summit stands at the top of this snowbank. But each time we reached that elevation, the trail snaked back across the ridge side, up another embankment.

Victor, however, was unperturbed. Every now and then, he would look back at me and say something to the effect of: "It's tough going, but where else could you see this?" Then he would throw his arms open, as if bringing the entire snowcapped panorama under our auspices, and I had to admit, I had never seen anything like it.

At around six o'clock, we finally climbed out of the snow, onto a nearly level ridge that led to the summit. I could see a badly weathered Norwegian flag flapping above our destination, the mountain hut called Fannarakhytta. Suddenly, we were joined from the other side of the mountain by a small group of British tourists. I was startled to hear more than one person speaking English, and we all marched together across a sea of igneous gray rock.

The hut itself was a modest wooden structure that had once been a weather station. In 1926 it was converted into a bunkhouse for the most intrepid of Norwegian wanderers. Taped to a wall inside the hut's small foyer, Victor pointed out a recent *New York Times* article that had named Fannarakhytta one of the ten most remote "hotels" in the world. Across the room, the hut's attendant, a good-humored young man, was busy checking hikers in.

The Norwegian Mountain Touring Club has an admirable system for housing its guests: there are no reservations; children and the elderly get the first beds, then women, then men. Obviously, at this elevation, no one is turned away. But a lot of younger people end up sleeping on the kitchen floor.

I approached the small wooden counter where the attendant stood, clipboard in hand.

"Do you have a sleeping bag?" he asked.

"Yes," I said. He checked a column on his list.

"Thick or thin?"

"Thin." Another check. Then he wrote down one word, which I hoped was the equivalent of "blanket."

"The best I can probably do for you is a foam sleeping pad," he said.

"Is it alright if I sleep outside?" I asked.

"That is what I would recommend."

A sign hung on the wall behind the him. It read:

FANNARAKA:

"GAA ALDRIG DIT . . ." —Ibsen

"What does that say?" I asked.

"Never go there," the young man replied. He smiled, then added, "The sign is meant to be ironical."

Some members of the British party were milling around us, pestering the attendant about water for their tea. He explained patiently, several times, that the kitchen could not spare any water because the closest spring was a quarter mile away.

I walked back outside. Three salubrious-looking young men came tromping up the summit. Then, on a patch of snow, they threw together two tents faster than I had ever seen tents assembled. More hikers arrived from the other side of the mountain. All the Norwegian men were tan and shirtless like Victor. The women wore little more. Everyone seemed quite at home in their skin. Except for the British, who were bustling about in long-sleeve, button-down shirts, still conferencing on where to locate water for their tea.

I found myself feeling ashamed of my fellow English speakers. Here at the summit, they didn't seem to be showing the proper respect for Mount Fannaraki. In fact, they hardly seemed to see it at all. I wanted to cast my lot with my great-grandmother's people, these rugged lovers of mountains.

I located a nice flat rock that tilted slightly toward the western horizon and dropped my pack there. The light had taken on a silver hue. The top of Mount Fannaraki felt like that most elemental of landscapes—rock married to sky. There were no intermediaries. Except of course us, the talking animals who had invented the words *rock* and *sky*.

The philosopher's first question, "Why is there something instead of nothing?" seemed irrelevant at the top of Fannaraki. Here, the fundamental metaphysic was that there *is* something—these irrefutable mountains—instead of nothing, and that something seems like its own kind of miracle. *Why?* It is a question that seems to rise only out of dissatisfaction with one's lot, one's place in the world, yet it reaches back to the very first landscape, the Garden of Genesis. Eve didn't ask it until the serpent made her doubt her place in that garden. And seventeen books of the Bible later, it was Job's fundamental question as well: Why? But when God finally got around to an answer, the voice of the whirlwind told Job, in blistering terms: *Who are you to ask? Before my vast creation, you are nothing— stop bothering me.* That is the real message of Job—not patience but modesty before the mystery of the Creator and the creation. And it's the message here too. The mountains don't need us; we need them, and we need a language of belonging to understand our presence among them. Whatever human culture might take hold in the Jotunheimen—say in the form of people gathering and telling stories at mountain huts—it could only be defined by the demands of the mountains themselves. The mountain seems to say: Forget the *why;* begin with the concrete miracle of rock and soil. Go from there.

———

Around seven or eight, all the hikers crowded into the dining room, where windows opened onto three views of the mountains—east, west, and south. I sat at a cloth-covered table with three Brits, a young Norwegian woman, and the three young tent builders, who turned out to be economists from Oslo. Casually, hospitably, the Norwegians switched all of their conversation into English.

"You picked the perfect time to come to Fannaraki," one of them told us. "It's foggy and rainy here three hundred and sixty days a year."

The hut attendant was suddenly standing at our side. With one finger raised, he said in a mock-serious tone, "Actually, that is incorrect. It is foggy three hundred and two days of the year."

The whole room broke up over that, and then we all got down to our plates of meatballs, cabbage, and flat bread.

All food is brought to Fannarakhytta by helicopter, but I don't think that limits the menu much. Norwegian cuisine seems wonderfully self-limiting. In every town or hut I traveled through, breakfast was the same cold cuts, jam, and hard-boiled eggs; dinner was the same cabbage-assisted beef dish (sometimes preempted by a cabbage soup). It's as if the entire country just gave up on the culinary arts about a thousand years ago. In Norway, the purpose of food is sustenance; end of story. A Frenchman searching for a wine shop or a decent meal would go out of his mind here, and the Norwegians probably view the French as hopelessly effete, the same people who thought up the Maginot Line. It isn't, I don't think, a matter of judgment really, but simply a question of what a particular culture chooses to value. In Norway, it's mountain huts; in France it's wine shops. Still, I admired how closely the Norwegians have aligned their definition of culture to their understanding of nature. They seem to have never forgotten that the word *culture*, in most languages, derives from the Latin *cultus*, meaning to dwell close to the land.

As it turned out, the prime minister of Norway, Jens Stoltenberg, was also off hiking that week, and a rumor was quickly moving around the dining room, at least among the British, that Victor was the prime minister. He had put on a button-down shirt for dinner, combed his hair, and exchanged his sunglasses for bifocals. He did, I had to admit, look rather ministerial.

Still, I told the English speakers at our table, "I hiked with him most of the day. I think it would have come up."

"But no," said one woman, "that's just it. He went hiking to get away from all that."

This back-and-forth went on for about a minute until one of the economists finally announced, "That is *not* our prime minister."

A bit grudgingly, the Brits admitted that a Norwegian might be able to recognize his own head of state.

I mentioned a newspaper article I had recently read that named Denmark as the world's "happiest country." What was the difference, I asked, between Norwegians and their southern neighbors?

"They come from villages and are used to sticking together," the Norwegian woman said. She was an architect who had lived for six years in Copenhagen. "They are more social. Norwegians believe in 'one man, one mountain.' Our country is very remote, so people never formed that collective feeling the Danes have. You know, it's good and it's bad."

Good in the sense that one learns self-sufficiency when living remotely—at least that's what I surmised—bad in the sense that we are, most of us, social animals after all. The Norwegians had their *friluftsliv,* their free-air life, and the Danes had their cigarettes and their convivial natures.

I asked about Arne Naess.

"Oh yes, he was very respected in Norway," said one of the economists. "His nephew was a mountain climber too. He married Diana Ross."

"Really?" I said.

"Yes, only he died in a climbing accident a few years ago. But he was quite famous, like his uncle. I mean, Diana Ross!"

I smiled at the unexpected synchronicity of our two cultures meeting symbolically through the marriage of the mountain climber to the Motown singer. Popular music is, alas, one of the few elements of American culture that Norwegians have chosen to appropriate. It would be nice, I thought, to see Americans appropriate Norway's *friluftsliv*—a love not only of one's country but of one's countrysides.

Around ten P.M., the hut attendant gave me the last of the foam sleeping pads, about four inches thick, and a blanket. I went off to claim my own part of the mountain for that evening. Nearby, two Norwegian girls sat on their own rock, braiding one another's hair. I unrolled the foam pad on my rock and settled in to watch the sun finally set behind the jagged western range of the Jotunheimen. The other forty or so hikers did the same. The blue-gray mountains were now turning to silhouette, and their own stark presence gave way to that even older deity, the sun. It cast a diffuse yellow glow across the horizon, then darkened to bright orange along the erratic contour of the farthest ridgeline. That orange swath stretched almost all the way around to the eastern mountains behind us. A deep quiet that seemed grounded in reverence settled over us all.

Slowly, the evening grew colder, until I realized that I was wearing, in multiple layers, every piece of clothing I had brought with me. The last thing in my pack was a four-ounce bottle of aquavit, a Norwegian liquor that I raised in salute to these ancestral mountains. As the harsh spirit warmed my chest, I spotted Victor at the edge of a precipice and walked down to where he was sitting. Together we pondered the last light as it disappeared behind those distant peaks.

"This is the most beautiful sight in Norway," he finally said.

"I absolutely believe you."

"Don't ever come back here!" he added with sudden conviction. "It will never be like this again. This is how you must always remember Mount Fannaraki."

And I thought: That's right. I won't ever come back. Instead I will let this day stand out in my memory, singular and luminous. And I realized Victor was right for another reason, one he couldn't have suspected. I had, as it were, traced my family's bloodline upstream, all the way to the top of this mountain in Norway. But now I had to follow its migratory path, as my family had, back to my real home in Kentucky.

I could see from the perspective of Mount Fannaraki what the Norwegians, with their impeccable environmental record, could teach us: to distrust corporations, to think of our grandchildren's generation, to adopt principles of modesty and empathy. That was certainly in keeping with the sermons my grandfather used to preach in his country church. The tenets of deep ecology didn't seem so different from the message in the Sermon on the Mount or the lessons of Job.

What was different was my own country's indifference to the size of its carbon footprint—the world's largest—and its indifference to the leveling of mountains to extract that carbon. In Norway, I had escaped that denial for a time, but to keep trying to escape it would only make me complicit in the denial. I had to go back. I had to return to Kentucky and try to be of use in the fight to preserve the mountains of my home state. Perhaps I could conjure some of that Viking tenacity that my grandfather said flowed through our family's veins. After all, even the peaceable Jesus had taken on the money changers in the temple, and it is money—"the root of all evil"—that corrupts the politicians and the coal operators back home. They had to be confronted. But, I thought, a successful resistance to their callous aggression must rise out of an impulse truer than theirs. That resistance would have to begin with reverence for what Henry Thoreau called "the poem of creation." It is an impulse that has nothing to do with money or self-interest and everything to do with humility and wonder in the presence of rock and sky.

LIONSPEAK

If the lions had been the painters it would have been otherwise.

—Henry David Thoreau

THE PHILOSOPHER LION

Among philosophers, literary critics, animal trainers, and gnostic proselytizers, there has been a lot of talk lately about talking lions. Sooner or later, most of this talk gets around to the gnomic philosopher Ludwig Wittgenstein, who had this to say on the subject: "If a lion could talk, we could not understand him." To me, this sounds something like that famous line from Wittgenstein's *Tractatus*: "Whereof we cannot speak, thereof we must be silent." These sentences are like two facing mirrors, each reflecting the other's emptiness. One sentence says, *There are things to know, but we cannot say them,* while the other suggests, *There are things to say, but we don't know what they are.*

FORTUNATE SON

Of course, Wittgenstein's sentence about the lion is a parable, complicated by paradox. Which makes it sound a lot like something that might have been said two thousand years ago in lower Galilee, by a figure as given to epigram as Wittgenstein and every bit as mysterious. In fact, the man we call Jesus did say something about the nature of lions and the nature of humans, and it does sound as cryptic as Wittgenstein's remark. In the apocryphal "Sayings Gospel," attributed to Judas Thomas the Twin, we find this:

> Jesus said, "Fortunate is the lion that the human will eat, so that the lion becomes human. And foul is the human that the lion will eat, and the lion will become human."

> [trans. Marvin Meyer]

In both cases, whether the man eats the lion or the lion eats the man, the result is the same—the lion becomes human. But with this difference: The man who consumes a lion profits from something the lion bestows—he becomes in some sense lionhearted—whereas the lion that eats a man becomes contaminated, befouled, by something within the man. What is it? "Sin" would be an obvious answer, except that the Gospel of Thomas hardly mentions the word. Indeed, the Jesus portrayed through these 114 sayings is distressingly, at least to mainline Christianity, unconcerned with *saving* humankind from Adam's congenital sin, which is probably why mainline Christianity has found no use for this extraordinary gospel. The human that Jesus speaks of here is not so much *fallen* and thus incontrovertibly tainted by sin; rather the human has become divided against his own nature. Thus the Jesus in the Gospel of Thomas exhorts his followers to search for some original self. Which is where the lion comes in. Jesus's lion, like Wittgenstein's, knows something that human beings have forgotten.

DON'T GET NERVOUS

The late poet Vicki Hearne was probably one of the few people who spent as much time talking to lion trainers as she did thinking about Wittgenstein's lion. Hearne herself trained dogs and horses and was the author of a book of essays called *Animal Happiness*. In her years of work with animals, Hearne wrote that she recognized "a strong sense of something else being recovered, not innocence, but knowledge that is *unmediated* and therefore not so nervous." Because animal knowledge has not reached the level of self-consciousness, it is an intelligence of a far different order than ours. The animal exists outside of historical time, free (as far as we call tell) of the fear of death, inseparable from being. It lives undivided, and the world has its undivided attention.

APOLLINAIRE

Qu'ai-je fait aux betes theologales de l'intelligence?

VOICE IN THE WILDERNESS

There is no narrative in the Gospel of Thomas, just as there probably was none in any of the earliest Gospels (which may account for why the parables of Jesus take on radically different meanings depending on the context in which the Gospel writers place them). Therefore, within the vast lacuna of Thomas, let me propose this set-piece:

After the Galilean wanderer was baptized by Johanan the Dipper, he emerged from the Jordan River and walked out into the Perean desert. There, amid the Golan Heights, he fell into a trance. The synoptic Gospels agree on this, though as usual, they offer little novelistic detail. I imagine Jesus sitting cross-legged in one of the small caves carved by wind and rain into that limestone ridge. I imagine him being visited by a talking lion, Wittgenstein's lion, who says:

> Images are visible to people, but the light within them is hidden in the image of the father's light. He will be disclosed, but his image is hidden by his light. . . .

> When you see your likeness, you are happy. But when you see your images that came into being before you and that neither die nor become visible, how much you will bear!

Jesus would later repeat these sentences to his followers, and one, Judas Thomas, wrote them down. Jesus's genius was that he understood the lion, though what the beast had to say could not be spoken in the usual language of images. Instead, the lion offers up what amounts to a Zen koan. And it was through this paradoxical notion of the face we had before we were born—the original imageless image—that this unlikely Galilean visionary suddenly perceived the true self that precedes form and transcends death.

One apocryphal source says that Andrew, the fisherman from Capernaum, rescued Jesus in his desert trance. Andrew had been a follower of Johanan, but when this stranger appeared on the banks of the Jordan, something about him made Andrew abandon the Dipper. Johanan had preached that the end of history was coming any day and that Yahweh would establish his heavenly kingdom on earth. But when Jesus returned with Andrew to Capernaum, he brought a different message:

> Jesus said, "If your leaders say to you, 'Look, the kingdom is in heaven,' then the birds of heaven will precede you. If they say to you, 'It is in the sea,' then the fish will precede you. Rather, the kingdom is inside you and it is outside you."

This is the theology Jesus learned from the lion. It is not enough to wait for the kingdom. We all have a spark of the original, divine light within us. That is why Jesus was always talking about lamps and lamp shades. By turning that internal light outward, we can see the world again for what it is: the earthly paradise, the kingdom of God. The lion is the opposite of the serpent. Where the serpent's *logic* leads the man and woman out of the garden, the lion's *Logos* leads them back.

SHAPE-SHIFTER

"Nietzsche walked in the Alps in the caresses of reality," Wallace Stevens remarked ruefully. "We ourselves crawl out of our offices and classrooms and become alert at the opera." When Nietzsche himself finally crawled away from his academic post at the University of Basel in 1879, it was in hopes of withdrawing into the mountains, "into the most shameless solitary existence." There Nietzsche created Zarathustra, the transcendent man, the whole man, who at age thirty left his own "home by the lake" to wander his own mountains and breathe the thin air of the higher man.

Bathed in the caresses of that reality, Zarathustra delivers his first sermon. Its theme is the metamorphosis of the spirit, from camel to lion to child. Zarathustra is speaking here of the *free spirit,* who must first bear up, like the camel, under the psychological duress brought on by refusing the common values of the villagers below. In the desert of this isolation, the camel is transformed into a lion that destroys his final god—the dragon named "Thou shalt."

> To create new values—that even the lion cannot do; but the creation of freedom for oneself for new creation—that is within the power of the lion. The creation of freedom for oneself and a sacred "No" even to duty—for that, my brothers, the lion is needed.

The lion must first destroy the culture of shame and its compulsory laws derived from the Tree of the Knowledge of Good and Evil. Only then will the spirit be free, not to impose a new system of values but to live *outside* all codes, in a natural realm that, in Heidegger's fine phrase, "lets Being—be." After the lion says no to all gods, to all doctrines, then he can say yes to Being.

And in saying yes, he is transformed into the child who does not judge the world but only *affirms* it. The child stands once more in a world that existed before the knowledge of good and evil. When the lion becomes a child, the story of exile ends, and the real poem of self-creation begins.

THE CURRENCY

In "Lions in Sweden," Wallace Stevens sounds as fed up with talking as the tight-lipped lion. He begins:

> *No more phrases, Swenson: I was once*
> *A hunter of those sovereigns of the soul*
> *and savings banks . . .*

Metaphor is the currency of the soul, just as a "sovereign," a coin, is the currency of the state, or worse yet, the savings bank. The Greek root of *metaphor* means "to transfer or carry." Carl Jung theorized that the highest symbol is a kind of pail dropped down into the psyche's murky depths; it retrieves and gives shape to the instinctual intelligence that exists—formless—within all of us. The lion is such a symbol. He embodies what we have lost in our evolutionary migration from nature to culture. "The whole of the soul," Stevens continues, "Still hankers after lions, or, to shift,/Still hankers after sovereign images." The problem is that even the lion as a symbol of the soul can be tamed, stripped of his power, turned into a tacky lawn ornament. In Stevens's pun, the "sovereign" becomes merely a "souvenir."

Indeed, the imagery of "Lions in Sweden," as well as its impli-cations, seems to rise directly out of Nietzsche's famous denial of truth:

> *Truths are illusions about which one has forgotten that this is*
> *what they are; metaphors which are worn out and without sen-*
> *suous power; coins which have lost their pictures and now matter*
> *only as metal, no longer as coins.*
>
> [trans. Walter Kaufmann]

"Truths" are only metaphors that have lost their power and mystery; they have fossilized into literal expectations, actual "kingdoms of God." The point for Stevens, as for Nietzsche, is not to discover the truth about the soul but to find new metaphors that will once more charge the soul with meaning. Poetry must keep *current* the soul's currency. If the lion is a dead metaphor, concludes Stevens, well, "The vegetation still abounds with forms." Just look at a painting by Henri Rousseau.

THE COWARDLY LION

The Gospel of Thomas is often called a "gnostic Gospel." There is still much contention as to what exactly *gnostic* means and whether Thomas's Gospel fits the criteria. But one indisputable character-istic of gnostic tractates is that they usually claim to reveal hidden teachings. And on closer consideration, one often sees that this par-ticular teaching is hidden not in the gnostic text itself but within the *person reading the text*. One dramatic saying from the Gospel of Thomas reads:

Jesus said, "If you bring forth what is within you, what you have will save you. If you do not have that within you, what you do not have within you [will] kill you."

In this sense, *The Wizard of Oz* can be read as a particularly gnostic fable. The Cowardly Lion already possesses the courage he is looking for, just as the Tin Man, who thinks he doesn't have a heart, is constantly crying (and rusting) over his friends' misfortune. But neither *knows* he already possesses what he seeks. They embody a typically American inclination to look anywhere for the remedy to personal anxiety except within one's self. The Wizard represents a sort of gnostic Christ figure, revealing to the seekers their true selves. He makes it clear to the Lion, the Scarecrow, and the Tin Man that the things he gives them—a diploma, a plastic heart, a medal—are only tawdry symbols of what they already possess. But like Jesus's followers, Dorothy's companions remain clueless to the end. The Cowardly Lion dances around with an iron cross pinned to his chest, the same comically unterrifying creature he has always been. Only Dorothy has discovered the secret, the *gnosis,* that will get her home: "If I ever go looking for my heart's desire, I won't look any further than my own backyard. Because if it isn't there, I never really lost it to begin with."

"Is that right?" the Tin Man asks Glinda the Good Witch.

"That's all it is," Glinda says brightly.

"That's so easy," gasps the Scarecrow.

To find the self that was never lost: the easiest and the hardest thing of all.

WHAT THE LION SAID

In Henri Rousseau's famous painting *Sleeping Gipsy* (1897), a wandering minstrel has fallen asleep on the desert floor. The moon is full. The mountains in the background look not unlike the white peaks of the Lebanon range where Jesus wandered for thirty days and thirty nights. To the left of the gypsy lies a mandolin. Over her right shoulder stands a male lion, who looks as if he is trying to sniff the sleeper's purple hair. But really, I think, he is bending down to whisper Wittgenstein's inexplicable sentence into her ear. It is the sentence that will return the wandering gypsy to her original homeland, to her original nature, to the face she had before she was born.

PRACTICE RESURRECTION

After a spring rain, the creek that runs below my house sounds raucous, suddenly full of purpose. It moves now like an animal furiously searching out its own disappearance into the Kentucky River a few miles away. On my walk this morning, I found a spool of barbed wire dangling from the branch of a fallen tree that hangs over the creek. It had been wound up to look like a contemporary crown of thorns. Last night's rain must have washed it down from one of the farms upstream, but the timing lends to it a rather sinister symbolism. The fact that it appeared during the last week of Lent gives me the uneasy feeling that this barbed wire crown was meant for me to find—a cosmic insistence that I believe in something I can no longer accept: the Easter miracle.

I always grow slightly uneasy this time of year because nothing measures the distance between my family's beliefs and my own so much as Easter. Like most mainline Christians, my family's version of Christianity is based on the idea that Jesus's crucifixion was not simply the execution of a subversive radical but rather an intentional act of martyrdom, a blood sacrifice meant to cleanse them of their sins and secure for them eternal life in the hereafter. When I was growing up, Easter Sunday always meant a new, two-piece polyester suit for me and a great feast for my family after church. As Christians, this was the most important day of the year for us, more important than Christmas or birthdays. The life of my family revolved around our Baptist church, and the life of that church revolved around this one event: the resurrection of Jesus into the saving Christ. Every few years, my parents gave me a new Bible for Easter, but really, the contents of those fourteen hundred pages could have been reduced to one passage, John 3:16: "For God so loved the world that he gave his only begotten son that whosoever believeth in him shall not perish, but have everlasting life." Nothing else really seemed to matter much. Everything Jesus did during his lifetime—the miracles, the healings, the proclamations, the driving of money changers from the temple—was all meant to *prove* he was the Messiah, the one who could forgive sin and break down the wall between life and death.

As I grew older, I found that I could no longer accept this version of Christianity. I never had a sudden epiphany like Paul on the road to Damascus, an *anti*conversion experience. Instead, my religion vanished like a mist off the creek. I'm not sure exactly when it disappeared, but I knew it was gone for good. I could no longer make the leap of faith. After all, aside from the obvious fact that no human being had ever risen from the dead, why had Jesus *waited so late* in human history to bring about this saving act? What about all the men and women who had lived before him? Were they all doomed to eternal darkness, or worse, hell? Wouldn't a just God have sent his son during the first generation of human beings? And couldn't He have sent him to a place a little less remote than Galilee, a poor Palestinian fishing village? Gradually, these questions were replaced by a more political one: Why had Christianity focused so much on

Jesus's death at the expense of his actual teachings? It's as if all we remember of Martin Luther King Jr. is that final night at the Lorraine Motel and nothing of his "Letter from Birmingham Jail" or his speech at the Lincoln Memorial that changed the direction of this country. Jesus, like King, was a martyr who died; that is true. There are neutral sources that attest to his crucifixion by Pontius Pilate. But, I concluded, Jesus died not to forgive future Christians of their sins or to save them from damnation but because he preached a radical message of egalitarianism that posed a serious challenge to the Roman Empire, just as King's message posed a serious challenge to the American Empire.

But because the majority of American Christian churches either ignore or minimize Jesus's social message, they have grown complaisant. I would go so far as to say they have become un-Christian, ignoring the words of Jesus for those of Paul and John, men who never actually knew the historical Jesus and who made his original teachings virtually unrecognizable. The problem with Jesus's actual message, his actual vision, is that it is nearly impossible for the average American to follow. And so we reject the historical walking and talking Jesus for the Christ who would absolve us of our mortal fears—and our worldly responsibilities. If the poor will earn their just reward in heaven, why fight for it here on earth? If a sky god will rescue us from this fallen world, why work to remediate its toxic air, soil, and water; why try to alter climate change? The Christ is a far easier figure to believe in than the historical Jesus. The Christ requires nothing of us but an amorphous faith that he was the only son of God. The historical Jesus requires that we change our lives in almost every way. Only then will we enter the kingdom of God.

What's more, the historical Jesus has been obscured and clouded over by the Gospel writers, who also never knew him and who exaggerated his accomplishments and distorted his sayings for their own political and eschatological purposes. After all, if Jesus had really raised the dead and walked across the sea, certainly Jewish or Roman historians would have made note of those miracles. They did not. It's as if the authors of Matthew, Mark, Luke, and John were playing a game of telephone as they drifted further and further from the original followers of Jesus. Thomas Jefferson was certainly one of the first Americans to sense this when he wrote that to truly understand the teachings of Jesus, one must extract "the diamonds from the dunghill." The dunghill was the gospellers' distortions, and so over a few nights in 1820, he took a penknife to the New Testament and excised a Jesus who performed no miracles nor rose from the grave. In doing so, Jefferson set in motion a long tradition of New Testament scholarship that sought to find the real Jesus beneath all the Christology and mythmaking.

I confess that I have been obsessed with such textual archaeology as well. Because I rejected the Christ sometime during college, it seems that I have become determined in my adult years to find the original, historical Jesus. It's ultimately an impossible search, of course. Jesus wrote nothing down—he was almost certainly illiterate. Nor did he speak Greek, the language of the New Testament. Still, there are ways to distill a more accurate portrait of this Mediterranean wanderer than what we find in the Gospels. One way to begin is with what scholars call "multiple independent attestation." That simply means: If you can find more than one independent source for something Jesus said, there's a higher probability that he actually said it. And if it comes from an earlier text, there's a higher probability still.

This is what twenty-first-century New Testament scholars know: Mark was the earliest of the four canonical Gospels, written around 70 CE. Matthew and Luke both borrowed from Mark—that's how we know it came first—but they also agree on a lot of information that isn't in Mark. This led scholars to "discover," embedded in Matthew and Luke, another, earlier text they call Q (from the German word for "source," *quelle*). Q dates to around 50 CE, and it is essentially a collection of pithy things Jesus said. Skeptics doubted that such a "Sayings Gospel" existed in the first century and thus doubted the actual existence of Q until a strikingly similar text, the Gospel of Thomas, was discovered in 1945. Not only are both Sayings Gospels, but they consist of many of the same sayings. The way double independent attestation works is this: If you can find a saying repeated in Mark, Q, Thomas, or John (an outlier that has almost nothing in common with the synoptic Gospels), there's a good chance Jesus actually spoke those words.

What kind of portrait emerges if we look at only multiple attestation? We find a man who is baptized by John and, after John's arrest by Herod, begins his own teaching, one quite different from John's. He is an itinerant teacher and welcomes to his table prostitutes, tax collectors, and other undesirables in Jewish society. He is a physician of the body and the soul, a healer and an exorcist, but his powers work only on those who truly believed in them. He is not at all interested in some coming apocalypse, and he emphasizes that there will be no sign from heaven of one. (That saying has more multiple attestations than any other in the Gospels.) Nor does he have any interest in his own messianic status, and when followers call him the Messiah, he denies it at every instance, except in John's Gospel, which bears little resemblance to the others. He is a man who teaches almost exclusively in aphorisms or parables that call into question the ways of the world. He espouses a kingdom of God—or more accurately an empire of God—that is the opposite in every way of the Roman Empire, or even the Jewish temple state. To enter this kingdom, one must first abandon one's family; Jesus is unequivocal about this. One must be humble and magnanimous because in God's kingdom, the last shall be first. One must forgive debts because the forgiving will be forgiven in the kingdom of God.

One must stop trying to find the sliver in a neighbor's eye when there is a plank in one's own. One must stop standing on empty ceremony, because God doesn't care what the outside of the cup looks like; it's the inside that matters. By the same token, it isn't what goes into one's mouth that matters but what comes out. And those words must be matched by deeds: a tree will be known by its fruit, and no one hides a lamp under a bushel. Therefore we must love our enemies and return violence with peaceableness. We must treat others the way we wish to be treated ourselves. We must be merciful.

Because so few of us are truly capable of these things, the kingdom of God is hard to find. The harvest is plentiful, but the workers are few. The rich will not find it because a man cannot serve two masters, God and mammon. There are no bankers in the kingdom of God because lending with interest—usury—is forbidden. The kingdom of God looks nothing like the kingdom of commerce—that was fundamental to Jesus's message. It was a kingdom for outsiders. Only they could see the radical, anarchic vision he put on offer. In Jesus's parable of the dinner guests, a man throws a banquet, but his affluent friends are all too busy to attend. So he sends out his servants to invite the poor in the streets. That's who will enter the kingdom of God: the destitute, the hungry, the suffering.

Where exactly is this kingdom? It is standing right before us. It is at once within us and outside us. To find it in one of these places is to see it equally manifest in the other. Yet though the kingdom of God is all around us, we are blind to it because our hearts are hardened, our minds preoccupied with worldly wealth and status. Our spiritual poverty exists in direct proportion to our economic wealth (and, I would add, our ecological abuse). But the kingdom is like the smallest seed, the mustard seed, that soon takes over an entire field. Jesus has cast a fire onto the world, he tells his followers, and he is waiting for the world to burn with that fire. Then we will see the kingdom of God.

That's it: that's the Jesus we find when we hold to the scholarly standard of multiple independent attestation. He is not a savior but rather an exemplar. He looks more like Diogenes, the Cynic sage, than like the founder of a new religion. Like Diogenes, he could not abide hypocrisy in any form and he found true freedom in a wandering, property-less life. In that he was also like John the Baptist. But whereas John prophesied a *coming* kingdom, Jesus said that it already existed, if we could only see it. We don't need to be saved or transfigured by Christ; rather we need to see that if Jesus can transfigure himself and the world, so can we all.

I have no training in scriptural exegesis. Everything I've just said comes from my own amateur bibliography—from putting the formula of multiple attestation to the test, a test I borrowed from brilliant New Testament scholars like John Dominic Crossan, Steven Paterson, Helmut Koestler, and John Kloppenborg. But based on that, I believe one can find a truer, more historically accurate account of who Jesus was and what he actually said by looking at such a portrait. The problem is that this isn't the Jesus most American Christians want to believe existed. His program is simply too demanding—and there's no reward of eternal life at the end. Instead, to those who followed these teachings, Jesus promised a *realized eschatology,* the transformation of one's life—*here, now.*

What all my research into the historical Jesus has led to is this conclusion: If Americans want to call themselves Christians, they should stop *waiting* for the kingdom of God promised in John 3:16 and start working to bring it about—by following the radical teachings of an itinerate Mediterranean street preacher named Jesus.

A few years ago, around this time of year, I wrote a short opinion piece called "Forget Easter" for the *Washington Post.* As above, my basic argument was that mainstream Christianity has made a huge mistake to focus so much on Jesus's death and so little on his actual teachings. My piece was not well received, if blogs, letters, and message boards are any indication. Many went to great lengths to point out the error and heresy of my ways. The president of the Baptist seminar in my hometown went on his radio show and denounced me as a postmodern heretic. I expected all that, more or less, though I wish one of my mother's church friends hadn't called to tell her about the radio show. What I didn't expect is that the piece would be picked up by the *China Times,* which translated it into ideograms that were, in fact, very well received. The general response to the piece in China was that I wasn't a Christian at all—but a Buddhist.

The American Christians who rejected my version of Christianity wanted a religion of revelation, and I was proposing a religion of experience. That, according to the philosopher Nietzsche, *was* a Buddhist approach, since Christianity always promises the former and Buddhism the latter. But that religion of revelation betrayed the true message of the historical Jesus. He didn't claim to forgive sins or be the Messiah; he didn't promise that his death would be a blood sacrifice to earn his followers life after death. That all came later, added by evangelists who clearly needed Jesus to be something he was not. In the end, Jesus wasn't a Buddhist any more than he was a Christian; he was rather a man who had recognized the stirrings of the holy within his own heart, and he turned that understanding like a mirror onto the world. Any of us could do the same. We don't need salvation from this world; we need to see this world for what Jesus said it is—the kingdom of God.

An entire ethics would follow. We would become stewards of that kingdom, the natural world, and we would enact Jesus's politics of radical empathy. The world as we know it would cease to be. Our days would burn with a beautiful intensity. We would live inside the resurrection.

THE CIRCULATORY SYSTEM: A MANIFESTO

On a clear July day, I climb to a prospect in the Adirondack Mountains called Castle Rock. A few clouds cast their shadows over the spurs and valleys, while down below a series of blue lakes flows slowly east to Hudson Bay. I paddle a solo canoe across the nearest lake and beach it at a trailhead about a thousand feet below where I am sitting. Now, without knowing quite why, I am thinking of Friedrich Nietzsche, who spent his last sane years living in Turin, among mountains similar to these, where he invented his theory of *amor fati*—"the eternal return." We must, said Nietzsche, live each day in such a way that if, at the end, we are told to do it all over, endlessly, we would not curse the fates but dance for joy. I suppose I am thinking of Nietzsche because of the mountains, but also because I am staying for a month in a small attic room of a lodge that once belonged to a New York copper baron, and the room reminds me of the one Nietzsche rented during those lonely but productive years in Turin. With just a desk, a single bed, and a small bookshelf, my room looks like photos I've seen of Nietzsche's hovel.

There's a similar austerity to the room, and that, coupled with the view from Castle Rock, has put me in a philosophical mood, a mood that leads to this thought: the eternal return—that's what this lake and these clouds are all about. The clouds hover above the mountains, where they pour rain down into the headwaters, which follow streambeds down to the lakes, which wander east to the Hudson and then the Atlantic, where the water eventually evaporates and begins its cloud-borne journey back to these blue mountains, or others like them. *Amor fati*, a love of one's fate, the eternal return.

The human circulatory system works in similar ways: blood flows from the four-chambered human heart, carrying oxygen to every one of the body's cells, which Charles Darwin once described as "numerous as the stars in heaven"; the right side of the heart pumps red blood cells up through arteries to the lungs, the brain, and out to the limbs' furthest arterioles; then the oxygen-depleted blood passes into the veins, where it circles back to the heart, over and over. Sitting in the high reaches of the Adirondacks, I like this idea that the human body is its own kind of landscape, whose blood is born from the heart's dark valley and flows like rivers through a confederacy of the flesh. I also like Darwin's suggestion, his poetic implication that the body is in some way a microcosm, a kind of map or template, of the vast universe. It's an idea that has always resonated with the more subversive elements in the Western religious tradition. In the late twentieth century, Lynn Margulis and James Lovelock gave this speculative theory of correspondences some scientific heft by actually demonstrating that the atmosphere itself functions as a circulatory system for the planet, cycling carbon, hydrogen, nitrogen, oxygen, phosphorus, and sulfur to maintain the climate's stability. This view from space reinforced William James's earlier hunch that the earth is one organism ("one animal," said James), or at least it functions as one. Zooming back down from the planetary perspective, we can observe how individual ecosystems and watersheds also circulate energy within their geographical boundaries, just as every animal within that watershed pumps blood from the heart through the extremities and back. And every cell within that animal is a self-contained pocket of circulating energy, where bacteria form millions of cooperative units, just as they first did two billion years ago.

This last part represents the creation story of life, according to Margulis, and as ultra-skeptic Richard Dawkins has written, "Not only is it more inspiring, exciting and uplifting than the story of the Garden of Eden, it has the additional advantage of being almost certainly true." Margulis's story of biological origins is also inspiring because it reinterprets that much-contested phrase *survival of the fittest* to mean survival of those who *cooperate*. What's even more astonishing about Margulis's research is that it affirms early intuitive analogies about heavenly bodies and human bodies by showing symbiosis at both the microcosmic level of the cell and the macrocosmic level of the biosphere.

The circulatory systems of the planet, its ecosystems, its animals, and their cells are obviously all chemical or biological processes, but they strongly suggest that if the entire natural world operates like a single, healthy organism, perhaps we might do far better to apply these same principles to our economy, our communities, and our faltering American democracy. I am not suggesting that there is a *moral* to be found in nature so much as a survival guide, an evolutionary strategy. After all, the cells and organs within a body do not compete with one another—the notion is absurd. Yet if our country were an actual organism, we would have to conclude that it is an extremely sick one. This sickness is due in large part to a blockage, a constriction, within the circulatory system of the body politic. Capital—human capital, natural capital, social capital, and monetary capital—has ceased to circulate properly. I am a little uncomfortable with the abstract nature, as well as the politically ambiguous connotations, of the term *capital*. But I use it here because, in a Jeffersonian understanding of this nation's earliest aspirations, many of these forms of capital—clean air and water, good soil, trust between neighbors, good public education, dependable represen- tation in politics—belong to us inherently as *assets* derived from living in a republic. But that circulatory system based on egalitarian principles has been choked almost to death by a contemporary ver- sion of capitalism that instead spreads toxic waste, toxic energy, toxic securities, and toxic political money throughout the social, natural, and economic landscape.

Eventually I wander down the mountain and paddle back across the lake to my solitary room. I sit at its small desk beneath an open window and listen to a pair of loons cackling below, while in the fading light, the lake turns from blue to silver to slate. I try to hold two thoughts in my head: one is about the natural beauty of the Adirondack Mountains; the other is about twenty-nine coal miners killed two months earlier when a methane fireball ripped through mine shafts beneath a mountain range in southern West Virginia. Those men were on my mind a lot during the months before I drove from my home in Kentucky, where strip mine operators are destroying the mountains of central Appalachia, up to the Adiron- dacks. Because the Upper Big Branch Mine in West Virginia was owned by Massey Energy, a company with an abysmal safety record, I felt sure the deaths of those twenty-nine miners could have been prevented, and I felt sure their deaths had something to do with the way our industrial economy has betrayed the circulatory system that functions at every level of the natural world.

As it stands now, our industrial economy is the very opposite of a circulatory system: it is a linear process that often begins with the brutal extraction of finite resources and ends with some form of toxic waste—what economics textbooks call throughputs. When those toxic throughputs bleed into streams and private wells, economists refer to the harmful effects of drinking and bathing in that water as externalities—costs that are external to the polluter's price of doing business. That is to say, someone else pays the price. In Kentucky, communities living around strip mines pay a crushing externalized health cost because of poisoned streams, air laden with coal dust, and floods caused by mining. So while coal operators and their stockholders reap the wealth of strip mining, rural Appalachians reap its opposite—what John Ruskin aptly called "illth." This affliction can best be described by Garret Hardin's phrase "the tragedy of the commons." That which should be a shared natural inheritance—rivers, mountains, air—is polluted by so-called corporate citizens who privatize enormous wealth while they socialize the illth. Corporate vandals take what isn't theirs; then they pollute the commons with waste that should not be ours.

Sitting at my desk, I look through a folder of clippings I've been collecting since the Upper Big Branch disaster, and I find these numbers: in 2010, when the twenty-nine miners were killed, Massey Energy CEO Don Blankenship earned $17.8 million, along with a deferred compensation package valued at $27.2 million. That same year, Dr. Michael Hendryx of West Virginia University's Institute for Health Policy Research published findings that children born near strip mines are 42 percent more likely to have birth defects than children born in other rural parts of Appalachia. Why? Because Don Blankenship and others like him internalize the wealth that comes from coal mining while his employees and the people living in the coalfields are left to live and die among the externalized illth. That, to my mind, is the tragedy of the commons.

Strip mining in Appalachia is perhaps the most egregious, but far from the only example of corporations turning natural capital into a grave debt for the rural communities that Thomas Jefferson once thought would be the harbingers of a decentralized, self-reliant form of democracy—the best system of government the world had ever seen. What's more, corporations like Massey Energy have worked hard to destroy social capital by breaking unions and polluting the political process with their enormous financial resources. This has happened all across the country, where, over the past thirty years, union membership dropped from 30 percent to around 13 percent, even as corporations like Massey Energy spent more and more money on politics. Today they shell out $6 billion annually to employ thirty-five thousand D.C. lobbyists to protect their wealth. After the miners where killed at Upper Big Branch, the coal lobby doubled its political contributions to the tune of $6.4 million. As a result, Congress killed stronger mine safety legislation.

Consider what has been removed from circulation in this scenario. Money has been removed from a community and transferred to a corporate headquarters. That money in turn buys more political power, which then removes working people further from any meaningful political process. Meanwhile, the increasing mechanization of American industries has reduced the number of jobs for which workers must complete. That loss, coupled with the decline of unions, causes all manner of goodwill to disappear within working-class communities. According to the National Opinion Research Center, levels of trust in the United States fell from 60 percent in 1960 to less than 40 percent in 2004. Into that vacuum powerful corporations pour more money so that we, the general public, gradually relinquish the realm of government to those wealthy corporations—run by the now-famous 1 percent.

What I think we should pay closest attention to here is how the decline in trust—social capital—has been paralleled by a widening income gap in the United States—the upward distribution of financial capital. The United States currently has the largest income gap of any country in the northern hemisphere, and the largest income gap in this country's history, according to the 2009 census. When trust weakens and economic inequality widens, an epidemic of social maladies follows. Epidemiologists Richard Wilkinson and Kate Picket have recently shown that every single societal problem, *with no exceptions,* can be tied directly to income inequality. As a result, the United States has higher levels of mental illness, infant mortality, obesity, violence, incarceration, and substance abuse than all other countries north of the equator. And because of our dependence on fossil fuels, we have the worst environmental record on the planet. When the West Virginia miners died, they were digging coal that the rest of us consume twice as fast as Americans did in the 1970s.

Yet herein lies an important source of hope in this whole bleak story: while our consumption of resources has doubled, psychologists and sociologists can find little evidence that we are any more content than we were four decades ago. While American GDP has risen 80 percent since 1970, the Index for Social Health—a seventeen-indicator measurement including suicide rates, income inequality, and life expectancy—has fallen 45 percent. A graph that measures these two trends would look like a ski slope, with social health measured on the downhill run while GDP rises like the chairlift. If GDP were a reliable indicator of well-being, we would be in a world of trouble, given that Americans consume five times more resources than the earth can sustain. But a mounting body of research has begun to show how the industrial economy, which destroys the natural world, is not the economy we truly desire, and for one reason—it doesn't deliver on what Aristotle called *eudaemonia,* or well-being. This derives from what sociologist Robert Lane calls "warm interpersonal relations, easy-to-reach neighbors, encircling, inclusive membership and solid family life." Notice how such virtues owe nothing, or next to nothing, to the culture of accumulation or the industrial economy dictated by corporations. What makes this so important is that if individual satisfaction can be derived from a culture that generates less material goods, then economic activity can be decoupled (in the language of economists) from a system that is carbon-intensive and fatal for both the land and its people. At that point eudaemonia can be found. That is to say, it can be created in the commons, where real wealth—human and social capital, as well as monetary capital—begins to circulate again throughout communities and ultimately throughout the watershed where those communities exist.

In fact a watershed, with its natural circulatory system of energy, is the perfect model for a healthy community and a sustainable economy. A watershed, with its geographical boundaries, is by its very nature self-sufficient, symbiotic, conservative, decentralized, and diverse. It circulates its own wealth over and over. It generates no waste and does not externalize the "cost of production" onto other streams and valleys. In a watershed, *all* energy is renewable and all resource use is sustainable. Compare this to the most unnatural of landscapes, a strip mine, which causes erosion and flooding, despoils air and water, and ultimately leads to a climate crisis. The watershed, by contrast, purifies air and water, holds soil in place, enriches humus, and sequesters carbon. That is to say, a watershed economy improves the land and thus improves the lives of the people who inhabit that particular place. It is an economy based not on the unsustainable, short-sighted logic of never-ending growth, which robs the future to meet the needs of the present, but rather on maintaining the health, well-being, and stability of the human and the land community. In that, the watershed both symbolizes and enacts an entirely new definition of *economy*, whereby our American system of exchange, both of wealth and energy, is brought in line with the most important and inescapable economy of nature.

The watershed economy I envision would be driven by three objectives: (1) lessening and correctly accounting for damage to the natural world and the use of natural resources; (2) improving citizens' physical, social, and psychological well-being; and (3) democratizing wealth and by extension political power. In other words, all forms of capital—human, social, natural, and monetary—must begin to circulate again within the new watershed economy.

Perhaps the most inspiring aspect of this alternate paradigm is that we don't have to wait for politicians to act or for corporations to find a moral compass. Outside these vastly compromised institutions, we can begin reversing the tragedy of the commons by taking actions that will reclaim the commons. And those actions are most easily undertaken and most effective within the political as well as the geographical terrain of one's own watershed. Defining a community by the watershed's natural boundaries keeps its economy local and also allows the local economy to emulate the watershed's diversity and self-sufficiency. By producing the things it needs, and only after that importing what it cannot produce, a community retains the wealth it generates much longer. In doing so, it also better defends against predatory corporations that feel no responsibility to the community, or to protecting its land, air, and water. Such an economy would subvert and decentralize the power of large corporate polluters like Massey Energy while it shortened supply lines and therefore both produced and consumed less fossil fuel. The better a local economy can provide the goods and services a community needs, the less wealth gets siphoned off to corporate stockholders and the more power and wealth return to the local watershed.

The manufacturing jobs within such an economy would shift from resource-intensive industries to those that both profit from and support a sustainable economy—industries built around public transportation, redesigned cities and buildings, and the production and delivery of renewable energy. We know that the country is moving inexorably away from a manufacturing economy. The United States has lost 5 million manufacturing jobs between 2000 and 2015. Before he died, Steve Jobs told President Obama flat out that Apple products would never be made in America, and a few months later we learned why: he preferred a workplace where conditions were so abysmal, as in Apple's Chinese factories, that nets were strung all around the buildings to catch workers attempting suicide. Yet back in this country, we have tried to replace a manufacturing economy with a predatory financial system that has clearly demonstrated its own suicidal tendencies by creating worthless financial "products" and then betting on their failure. (This used to be called securities fraud; now it's called business as usual at Goldman Sachs.) In this scheme of things, for someone to make money, someone else must lose money. That fixed game must now succumb to an authentic economy that emphasizes real needs and desires. What we need is an economy based not on winners and losers but rather on reciprocal exchanges in which both parties benefit from the transaction. Such an economy would reduce ecological damage while building more convivial communities where social capital circulates alongside the dollars we spend locally. It would replace our current culture of accumulation with a needs- and service-driven economy that actually delivers on the promise of well-being instead of hocking flimsy substitutes made in China. And because a needs-and-services economy speaks directly to our sense of well-being without sublimating our desires through endless acts of material consumption, we would improve our physical and mental health while decreasing our destructive impact on the natural world.

The "service economy" I'm advocating here has nothing to do with low-wage jobs or unrewarding jobs in the fast-food industry but rather their opposite, such as a dynamic, locally run farmer's market like the one in my home of Lexington, Kentucky. I'm talking about jobs that cannot be outsourced and that contribute to the quality of a community. I'm talking about community bankers, teachers, health care workers, carpenters, mechanics, landscapers, plumbers, physical trainers, coaches, architects, engineers, jewelry makers, bus drivers, store owners, organic farmers, restaurateurs who serve locally grown food, musicians and artists, and the men and women who will build and supply local sources of renewable energy. Because such an economy rewards the services of those who add value to the community, and because so many of these exchanges involve mutually beneficial, face-to-face interactions, social capital—that is, good feeling and trust—would circulate alongside monetary capital. The commons would again expand, while economic aggressors would be driven from the marketplace.

However, when I return to my original objective of correctly accounting for damage to the natural world, I realize that this is one thing a watershed economy cannot do: It cannot force destructive corporations to act with anything resembling a collective conscience. It cannot force them to pay the true cost of their environmental damage. But this obviously must happen if we are to stave off the oncoming climate crisis and if we are to stop the damage done by mountaintop-removal strip mining, hydraulic fracking for natural gas, and the other nefarious effects of the fossil fuel industry. The problem is that Americans make up 5 percent of the world population but are responsible for 25 percent of the world's carbon dioxide emissions. As a country, we must quit pretending that natural capital is free. We must pay the true cost of carbon, and this can happen only at the federal and the international levels. The way to do this is simple enough in its conception, though politically difficult: We must make polluters pay for their deeds. We shift taxes away from "goods," such as income, toward "bads," like carbon and pollution. We must subsidize the things that encourage health and stop subsidizing things that encourage illth. Right now, as Arctic ice sheets are melting far faster than scientists predicted, the most practical lever for realigning the economy and for making polluters pay the true cost of natural capital is a cap-and-dividend tax on carbon.

Peter Barnes has made the winning suggestion that the best way, on the macroeconomic level, to counter corporations and protect the commons is with public trusts. The goal of the commons and the goal of a trust, he argues, are largely the same: to preserve assets and deliver benefits to a broad class of beneficiaries. Perhaps the most successful and well-known American trust of this kind is the Alaska Permanent Fund, which takes oil revenue and pays an equal annual dividend to every Alaskan man, woman, and child. Such a trust could be established to protect and manage any kind of common: a river, a forest, the recording industry. In his book *Who Owns the Sky?* Barnes ultimately envisions a Sky Trust that would solve the global climate crisis through a cap-and-dividend model that would require all fossil fuel companies to purchase emission permits from a trust representing every person on the planet. The trust's income would then be used to remediate damage done by climate change and to rebate individuals for higher energy bills. United Nations scientists would decide where to set a global cap on emissions, and rights to the atmospheric commons would be divided in proportion to each country's population—absolute equity. Poor and populous countries with more permits than emissions could sell their excess permits to richer nations. And if it all sounds too simple, it is worth noting that the Congressional Budget Office found that of all the cap-and-trade proposals put forward so far, the Sky Trust would be easiest to implement and would have the most positive effect on household incomes.

Today, the rich remain rich because they control the resources of the commons; the poor remain poor for exactly the same reason. The commons trust could go a long way toward solving the problem of inequality, not by *redistributing* wealth—that thing Americans can't seem to abide—but by *predistributing* it. After all, the natural wealth of the commons *already* belongs to everyone, or it should. It's only those who can turn a profit at the expense of the commons who convince us to think otherwise. But by providing access to the commons and paying equitable dividends for that access, we would, in Barnes's words, "produce the most happiness with the least destruction to nature." That would indeed go a long way toward ameliorating the pathologies of capitalism: gross inequality, unsustainability, third world poverty, and first world malaise.

The words *ecology* and *economy* both derive from the Greek root *oikos*, referring to the daily operations of a household, or as we used to say, home economics. In terms of climate change, we must start thinking of the atmosphere's thin membrane as the roof that now holds tenuously to our one planetary household. We must finally align our human economy with the symbiotic laws of the watershed. The fundamental tenets of nature's economy were set down sixty years ago by the great American conservationist Aldo Leopold: "A thing is right when it tends to preserve the integrity, stability and beauty of the biotic community. It is wrong when it tends otherwise." This clear and profound distinction between right and wrong, between the ethical and the unethical, can carry us quite far. Whenever we make a decision about our own human communities or about our human impact on the natural world, we should ask: Will this create or destroy the integrated nature, the stability, or the beauty of this place?

My contention is that the watershed economy better fulfills authentic human desires at the same time it makes us stewards rather than conquerors of the natural world. But the reality is that with nine million people on the planet in 2050, economic and political cooperation will *have* to win out over competition for limited wealth and limited resources. If in the end survival is the name of the game, that will be the best—by which I mean the only—solution to living in a finite world.

Now the sun has completely disappeared behind the mountains across the lake, and the only light I see comes from down at the boathouse, where a summer theater troupe is rehearsing a stage adaptation of Ovid's *Metamorphosis*. The actual production will take place in the boathouse, so the actors can perform part of the play in the water and part of it around the edge of the boat slips. Moving in and out of the water, they will presumably condense three billion years of evolutionary time—from the primordial soup to the boatbuilding hominid—into a two-hour performance. Their presence tonight reminds me that cooperation always played a much larger role in our evolutionary past than social critics have allowed. That is the reason democracy has a future and free market competition has been exposed as the serpent that eats its own tail. Looking down at the actors, sipping a glass of wine, I find it entirely possible to imagine a more sustainable economy and a more rewarding culture built upon the natural laws I first observed from the top of Castle Rock. I find it possible to imagine a new set of human values that cauterizes the linear flow of toxic waste, which ends only as wealth for the very few and illth for the rest of us. It is possible to imagine instead an economy that operates like a circulatory system, wherein the very idea of waste is eliminated and, as with Nietzsche's eternal return, all resources are recycled within a continual flow of natural, social, and human capital. The American poet Walt Whitman, frustrated by the "corruption, bribery and falsehood" of his own time, maintained late in life that democracy was still "a good word" whose fruition "lies altogether in the future." It lies there still, but the urgency to make it real has never been greater.

FLIGHT RISK

*A Journal from the One Hundredth Year
of Human Aviation*

In January 2003, an F-117 stealth bomber flew over the Wright
brothers monument at Kitty Hawk to celebrate the centennial anniversary of human flight. That same year, an aircraft carrier called the
USS Kitty Hawk arrived in the Persian Gulf, where it launched forty
Tomahawk cruise missiles meant to kill Saddam Hussein. Those at-
tacks were followed by around-the-clock bombing raids by fighter
jets launched from the flight deck of the *Kitty Hawk*. At the time, I
was following a website called Iraqibodycount, which reported that
between six thousand and seventy-eight hundred Iraqis—excluding
soldiers—had been killed by the American armed forces.

That same month, I cut out and pasted in my journal a small
newspaper picture, shot in profile, of a Polish girl at an antiwar rally
in Warsaw. She had painted bombs in place of tears falling down
her left cheek. Next to her picture, I wrote this from Henry Adams's

essay "The Law of Acceleration": "Bombs educate vigorously, and . . . airships might require the reconstruction of society." Adams wrote his essay at the same time Wilbur and Orville Wright were figuring out the science of human flight. Yet it is clear that Adams knew nothing of the Wrights' experiments, since by "airship" he meant a zeppelin held aloft by helium instead of a glider propelled by gasoline. But he did have the kind of mind that could leap ahead to a time when bombs and planes—and planes *as* bombs—would forever be linked. Nothing so much as the history of flight illustrates Adams's law of acceleration, which says that human civilization is careening into the future with an ever-increasing speed that we are powerless to stop. The speed by which technological society advances can be measured by squaring the achievements of the last generation—that was Adams's formula. There was unquestionably a "vertiginous violence" associated with such acceleration, said Adams, but he believed the modern mind could harness that force and use it for good. "At the rate of progress since 1800," wrote Adams, "every American who lived into the year 2000 would know how to control unlimited power. He would think in complexities unimaginable to an earlier mind."

But alas we don't, and we don't.

That first human flight actually took place on December 17, 1903. The Wright brothers had been in Kitty Hawk, North Carolina, since September, assembling the machine they had come to call the *Flyer*. By December, they were still repairing propeller shafts that had twisted loose under the torque of a grinding engine. Stores were running low: their supper was crackers; breakfast was rice cakes. On the twelfth, the shafts were finally ready. The thirteenth was a Sunday, and the brothers had promised their father, a retired bishop of the United Brethren Church, that they would keep the Sabbath holy. So on the fourteenth, they laid their sixty-foot launching rail down along a gently sloped dune. They flipped a coin, and Wilbur won the toss. He crawled into the hip cradle on the lower wing. Orville cranked the engine, and their mechanized bird, with its forty-foot wingspan and a gasoline engine, started down the runner. Six feet from the end of the track, the *Flyer* rose into the air. Wilbur had hoped to take it eight miles, to the village of Kitty Hawk. But he over-adjusted the elevator pulley, and the *Flyer* sank back to earth 105 feet from takeoff. As far as the brothers were concerned, this didn't count as flight.

The next two days were taken up with repairs to the undercarriage. Then, on the seventeenth, despite strong headwinds, Orville was eager for his turn between the diaphanous wings. Four men from a nearby lifesaving station came to watch. Orville settled into the cradle, and as the *Flyer* started forward, Wilbur ran alongside his brother, holding the right wing in balance. The *Flyer* rose again, tilted left, leveled out, dipped, rose, then dipped again, this time skidding into the sand. The flight lasted twelve seconds, reached an altitude of ten feet, and covered 120 feet.

Then, at high noon, Wilbur crawled back into the cradle. Again the *Flyer* rose, this time to fifteen feet, and again it began to pitch convulsively. It dipped to an altitude of one foot. But about three hundred feet from the start, Wilbur pulled the plane under control. It rose to ten feet and leveled off. He sailed for five hundred more feet over the open coast. This, unquestionably, was flight—the first human-powered flight in the history of the world.

One day when I was seven, I came home from school certain, for some reason, that I had solved the problem of motorless human flight. I cut a crude pair of wings from two plastic garbage bags and wrapped them around my arms. Then I climbed up onto the roof of my parents' house and jumped. Fortunately, we lived in a ranch-style house. I fell only about ten feet before landing in a dense row of arborvitae. When my mother saw the scratches on my face, I eventually confessed to my Icarian fall.

"If it was that easy," she said in disgust, "don't you think someone else would have already figured it out?"

In his journals, now lost, the French aviator Roland Garros wrote ecstatically about the strange longing in children to fly, perhaps to fly away. Flight is escape—either from the laws of gravity or from the laws of the tribe. Or the family. My family was made up of fundamentalist Christians, and gradually I would come to feel that doctrine pressing down on me like the most oppressive law of gravity. It took many years to unburden myself of those laws. I began searching noncanonical Christian texts for a version of Christianity that might not repulse me. One such text was the apocryphal Acts of Peter, where I discovered the arch heretic Simon Magus. No one in the literature of the New Testament—canonical and apocryphal— comes in for so much abuse. His sensuous cosmology seemed to me a healthy corrective to the asceticism and the piety of the Baptist churches I grew up on. It went like this: Out of an unfathomable silence—the source of all sources—there rose the mind (Nous), and out of the masculine mind sprang the feminine thought (Ennoia). From this androgynous coupling, the world came into being. But the creatures of the world famously misbehaved. Ennoia, therefore, descended to the world in an attempt to set things right. But instead, she was imprisoned inside the human flesh of Helena, the whore of Tyre, then later inside Helen, the instigator of much Greek misfortune. Nous then descended into the realm of being to reunite with Ennoia. Simon Magus claimed that he was Nous and that the questionable woman with whom he traveled was none other than Helen, Ennoia.

According to the Acts of Peter, Jesus's strong-willed disciple loathed the flesh as much as Simon Magus reveled in it. This became the basis of their antipathy. In one of Peter's earliest acts, a gardener asked him to offer a prayer for his only daughter, a virgin. Immediately, the girl fell dead. Peter explained to the grievous father that his daughter had been delivered from the "shamelessness of the flesh." But her father, failing to see the divine blessing in Peter's act, begged him to bring his daughter back to life. This Peter did, but only before ending his cautionary tale with this damning detail: a stranger soon visited the home of the old gardener and seduced his daughter. The two were never seen again.

But Simon Magus was apparently as skilled a sorcerer as Peter. He too could strike a boy dead by whispering in his ear, then bring him back to life, as he supposedly did in front of a coliseum crowd. But what really rattled Peter were the rumors coming from Rome that Simon could fly. And sure enough, when Peter arrived in Rome with the intent of exposing Simon for a sham, he met a large crowd that had gathered on the Sacred Way. They were all staring skyward, where Simon was at that moment doing figure eights above the plane trees. Occasionally he would dip down toward the crowd to hurl some invective at his rival. Peter, for his part, raised up a quick prayer, pleading with his lord that if Simon's flight was not immediately brought to a tragic halt, then all of Rome would be lost to Christendom. "Let him fall from this great height, Lord, and be crippled by his fall," Peter pleaded. And suddenly, like a glider hitting a crosswind, Simon plunged to earth. He broke one leg in three places, and when a doctor named Castor tried to operate, Simon did not survive the procedure.

It must be said, however, that Peter's victory in Rome proved short-lived. When he convinced the concubines of the prefect Agrippa to adopt a life of chastity, the prefect had Peter put to death.

So ends the Acts of Peter.

On the first day of the second Iraq War, I drove to the Daniel Boone Forest in eastern Kentucky and walked until that manmade thing, the state, disappeared and was replaced by chestnut oaks and sand-stone outcrops. I made my camp in a small clearing beneath the constellation Orion. I fell asleep listening to the barred owl and woke up to the distant drumming of the ruffed grouse. That drumming, in fact, might be a clue to how animals ever took to the air in the first place. A transitional fossil form that is half bird and half dinosaur was discovered in a German limestone quarry in 1860. Like the grouse's cousin the chukar partridge, the winged dinosaur may have used its wings for propulsion while running, until one day, when trying to run faster, it took to the air—first in short hops, like the Wright brothers, and then finally in a long careening glide.

Two things fascinate us about birds: they can fly and they can sing. No other animals really come close in either department. When the wood thrush, a bird with a beautiful song, migrates back to Kentucky, he flies by night, guided by the fixed north star and laminar winds. Then he waits for the female to arrive before he breaks into a tremolo that is purer than that of any other passerine that migrates to these deciduous woods.

Birds sing because they can, both physiologically and territorially. They have developed a sophisticated voice box, the syrinx. Though the song gives away their whereabouts, few predators can climb into the sky after them. They sing to woo and warn, to breed and defend territory. Each song is essentially an improvisation on the standard of that species, and the female will often choose her mate based on how eloquently he can improvise. Some ornithologists have even ventured out on a thin limb to suggest that birds sing because of sheer pleasure in the world as they find it at sunrise. What birds definitely do not sing is what W. E. B. Dubois called the sorrow-song. The mourning dove is not really mourning. The loon is not really going crazy from lovesickness. In Walt Whitman's eulogy for President Lincoln, "When Lilacs Last in Dooryard Bloom'd," a thrush has withdrawn into "the swamp in secluded recesses" to mourn the slain leader:

> *Song of the bleeding throat,*
> *Death's outlet song of life, (for well dear brother I know,*
> *If thou was not granted to sing thou would'st surely die.)*

But of course it is Whitman's heart that is bleeding, not the thrush's syrinx. Whitman, not the thrush, is singing death's outlet song. The thrush will not die if it doesn't sing, though he might die alone. Rather, it is our species that needs to shape heartbreak into something that will help us bear it. Only we, the animals who can comprehend our own death, hope for a savior we might rise up to meet "on the wings of a great speckled bird."

Perhaps song and flight are so intimately bound in our species-consciousness because we first learned to sing from the birds. Consider a Kaluli legend from Papua New Guinea in which a boy trolls for crayfish with his sister. She catches some; he none. The boy begs his sister for one of her crayfish, but she refuses. So the boy catches a shrimp and pinches it over his nose until it turns the reddish purple of the muni bird's beak. He stretches out his arms, which turn into wings, and the boy flies away. His sister begs her brother to come back, but he replies, "Your crayfish you did not give me. I have no sister."

The American poet Nathaniel Mackey has read into this story the origin of music. "For the Kaluli, the quintessential source of music is the orphan's ordeal," wrote Mackey. "Song is both a complaint and a consolation dialectically tied to that ordeal." The musical harmony replaces the social harmony that has been stolen from the estranged singer. And yet many anthropologists suspect that music, allied with the communal dance, first served the evolutionary purpose of establishing social harmony among *Homo sapiens* through acoustic harmony. In addition, the repetition of acoustic patterns made the tribe's stories mnemonically easier to remember. Still, at some point, that sense of belonging to the social unit is denied someone, such as the Kaluli boy, who then turns to a new song, the orphan's song—the blues. Such a song now becomes at once a cry of woundedness and a wanting to be taken back. Our words state the wound while the music heals it.

In their own hometown, the Wright brothers suffered the famous treatment of prophets. Five men had witnessed the first human flight at Kitty Hawk. The brothers telegrammed their father back in Dayton, Ohio, and told him to alert the media. But when Frank Tunison, the editor of the *Dayton Journal,* heard that Wilbur had flown for almost a minute, he was startlingly unimpressed. "Fifty-seven seconds?" he is reported to have said. "If it had been fifty-seven minutes, then it *might* have been a news item." In truth, the country had been waiting for Samuel Langley's experiments, funded by the War Department, to solve the problem of human flight. Soon Langley would be cata-pulting his flyers over the Potomac River, only to watch them dive ingloriously into the water. But that a couple of midwestern bicycle mechanics had beaten Langley into the air—certainly that was just another hoax.

After their return to Dayton, the brothers got the permission of Torrance Huffman to let them build a second *Flyer* on his farm on the outskirts of town, where they might perfect their circling techniques and lengthen their time in the air. Dayton's interurban trolley ran alongside Huffman's pasture, and from time to time, pas-sengers caught a glimpse of *Flyer* no. 2 rounding the large honey locust in the middle of the field. Still the press stayed away. The brothers stretched their flight time to five minutes, covering three miles of figure eights. According to Dayton journalist Fred Kelly, "Most of the long flights in late September and October, 1905, had been seen by Amos Stauffer, a farmer working in an adjoining field.

But he went right ahead husking corn." Apparently, if the fall of Icarus went unnoticed by Bruegel's plowman, so it seems did his ascent.

Sixty years ago, the inventor of modern French poetry, Blaise Cendrars, began writing again. He had stopped three years earlier after his son Remy, a pilot with the British Royal Air Force, was shot down and killed in the Battle of Stalingrad. A man suspected of Jewish sympathies, Cendrars escaped to Aix-en-Provence, where he hid in a room next door to a Gestapo informer. There Cendrars began burning all his papers, until it occurred to him that a writer with *no* evidence of writing would seem as suspicious as one hiding a manuscript of *Chez l'armee anglaise*. He began to visit the library in La Mejanes to give himself an alibi.

Three years earlier, when Remy had visited his father in Paris, Cendrars had gone looking for a saint's medal depicting Joseph of Copertino. Cendrars had decided that Joseph, a Franciscan monk who, it was said, had levitated more than seventy times during his life, would be the saint best suited to look after Remy.

But when Cendrars told Remy of his search for a Saint Joseph, Remy recoiled: "Oh, shit! The patron saint of exams!"

"The man himself," said Cendrars.

This requires some explaining. Joseph of Copertino was a cobbler's son. Of twelve children, Joseph was the only one who could not manage a decent boot. When one day Joseph nailed his thumb to the workbench, the cobbler dragged his son to the local monastery and pleaded with the Friars Minor to take him into their order as an oblate. The friars reluctantly agreed to accept Joseph and gave him the task of caring for the order's mule. This was 1625.

Joseph's acumen did not improve. Of all the prayers, the only word he could remember was "Amen!" Yet by some miracle, the Minor Conventuals of Osimo decided to admit Joseph as a novitiate.

Three years later, when it came time for Joseph to take the examination for admission into the priesthood, he simply replied, "Amen!" to every question. His examiners took this as a sign of unaffected profundity, and Joseph of Copertino was ordained a priest in 1628. As a result, and to Remy's horror, sometime over the next three hundred years, Joseph became known as the patron saint of exams. But even more curious is what happened after Joseph passed the exam. When he started home to tell his parents the news, Joseph suddenly felt his feet leaving the ground! In the next moment, he found himself floating in front of his disbelieving parents. Thinking that he had somehow embarrassed them, Joseph flew away.

Blaise Cendrars never found a Saint Joseph medal for Remy. But in September 1943, while in hiding, he came across a newspaper clipping that announced that Joseph of Copertino had been named the patron saint of American aviators. It was then, three years after Remy's death, that Cendrars began writing again. At the library in La Mejanes, he began sifting through hagiographies, trying to reconstruct the life of Joseph of Copertino.

After that first flight from his parents' house, Joseph joined the Franciscans at Assisi. There, the smallest thing, like the way light fell on a lamb's ear, could send Joseph airborne. Once he pulled a gardener up into the air with him, and the two of them spun there for several minutes above the anemones and hibiscus. Often, when reciting the liturgy, Joseph would rise up to the tabernacle and hover there until his superior ordered him down. One day, unaccountably, he flew into the refractory brandishing a sea urchin.

When it came to the attention of the Holy Office that Joseph had been preaching sermons on humility while hovering above an olive tree, he was summoned to Naples on "suspicion of wizardry." Standing before the judges, Joseph felt so unworthy that he tried to throw himself at their feet. Instead, he rose helplessly into the air until at last, he was bumping against the high ceiling, where he could no longer hear the accusations of his examiners. Nevertheless, they censured Joseph for the sin of pride and ordered him to retire to an isolated monastery at Fossombrone. People flocked there to catch a glimpse of the flying monk, and an entire town of hotels and taverns grew up around the monastery. Joseph was transferred from one cell of isolation to another, until he was eventually sent back to his original convent in Osimo, where he died in 1663 at the age of sixty.

Cendrars, for his part, eventually turned all the material he had gathered about Saint Joseph into a wartime memoir called *The Patron Saint of Aviation*. It is a collage text—part allegory, part elegy, part apocalypse. The saddest moment comes when Cendrars reads that the American flyers have adopted Joseph as their patron saint. "My dear little Saint Joseph!" he exclaims—by which we must understand him to have meant, "My dear lost Remy!"

Before a Parisian crowd, in October 1906, a Brazilian named Alberto Santos-Dumont flew a distance of seven hundred feet in a strange-looking contraption made out of box kite cells. Unlike Wilbur Wright's seven-hundred-foot flight three years earlier, news of this one spread quickly across Europe and to the United States. This time, President Roosevelt took note and suggested that his War Department reestablish contact with the two brothers from Ohio who said they had built a flying machine. In early 1908, a contract was written up: a trial flight would be held in September, and if it proved a success, the United States would pay $25,000 cash for one *Flyer*. The Wrights had also worked out a deal with France that would earn them $100,000 for one *Flyer* and lessons. An official French trial would be held in the fall. In this way, the brothers would simultaneously reveal their invention on two continents.

Wilbur arrived in France in May 1908. From the beginning, the Parisian press raised suspicions about the flights at Kitty Hawk and instead lauded the accomplishments of a Frenchman, Louis Bleriot, who had flown six miles in a single-wing craft. Wilbur set up shop at a racecourse in Le Mans, where he began to assemble the *Flyer*. But on July 4, while he was running the engine at 1,500 rpm, a hose burst and sprayed Wilbur's left arm with scalding water. The accident was reported in the papers, but Wilbur refused to show his wounds to photographers, leading to further speculation that the Wrights were mounting an elaborate hoax. Wilbur still let no one see the *Flyer*, and he slept beside it every night in the shed hangar to guard against interlopers.

Finally, at the beginning of August, Wilbur said that he was healthy enough to fly. On the eighth, papers announced that he might fly that day. Spectators began to fill the wooden bleachers early at the racecourse in Le Mans. Wilbur ordered the *Flyer* to be lifted onto the rails of the catapult that would launch his flight. Around five in the afternoon, he emerged from the hangar in a gray suit and tie. He climbed into the pilot seat, cranked the engine, and before the crowd quite realized what had happened, Wilbur Wright had shot into the air and was flying. A cheer went up. At thirty feet, Wilbur tilted the left wing by shifting his hips and banked for a tight turn. The crowd shrieked, thinking the *Flyer* was falling. But when Wilbur leveled off and sailed over the grandstand, wild cheering began again. (The next day he would perform a figure eight to even wilder applause.) Wilbur circled the racecourse a few times and then coolly landed *the Flyer*. The crowd flooded out of the stands to shake Wilbur's hand and shout congratulations. Louis Bleriot wandered among them, stunned and bewildered. Another Italian aviator, Leon Delagrange, who had once kept a lumbering plane up for fifteen minutes, told a reporter, "We are beaten! We just don't exist!"

Orville Wright succeeded his brother's triumph in France with a fifty-seven-minute flight over the army grounds at Fort Myer in

Washington, D.C., thus securing their American contract. Back in France, Wilbur extended the record to two hours and twenty minutes, at an altitude of 300 feet. When he landed, the French minister of public works told Wilbur that the French government would award him and Orville the Legion of Honor.

Back in Washington, on June 10, 1909, Wilbur and Orville were greeted by President William Howard Taft as guests of honor at the White House. Before an audience of a thousands, Taft praised the brothers' persistence and humility. He closed with the hope that the flying machine would be used for the benefit of all nations and not as an implement of war.

Cendrars, in *The Patron Saint of Aviation*, contended that Joseph of Copertino was the only saint to ever fly backward. While the hagiography does indeed bear this out, we might still give some philosophical consideration to another backward-flying enigma—Walter Benjamin's Angel of History. In his "Theses on the Philosophy of History," Benjamin meditates on Paul Klee's painting *Angelus Novus*, in which he sees an angel with open wings contemplating some object in the distance. This, Benjamin decides, is how we should imagine the Angel of History: wings spread, moving away from us, his eyes staring back. He is looking into the past. But "where we perceive a chain of events," wrote Benjamin, "he sees one single catastrophe which keeps piling wreckage upon wreckage and hurls it in front of his feet." The angel wants to return, to "make whole what is smashed." But a storm is blowing him into the future, and the storm is called Progress.

Klee's angel is to Benjamin what Joseph of Copertino was to Cendrars—a patron saint that cannot, ultimately, save us. The technological winds blow too strong. The angel has been replaced by the airplane, in which the poet's son is shot down by another airplane. The airplane comes to embody the Angel of History, carrying us so fast into the future that we can no longer stop to question the force that sweeps us along and goes by the name Progress.

In the most vivid dream I ever remember having, my grandfather the Baptist minister and I are arguing over the true message of the Gospels. He maintains that Christ died for our sins so that we might enter the kingdom of God. I say that the kingdom of God already exists, spread out before us, and we have only to recognize the holy within ourselves to enter it. My grandfather demands that I offer proof of my apostasy. To my surprise, I respond by rising into the air.

In the fall of 1909, New York City was planning to celebrate the three hundredth anniversary of the year Henry Hudson sailed his schooner the *Half Moon* into New York Harbor. A huge flotilla of naval vessels would parade along the Hudson River. The world's most famous ship, the *Lusitania*, was scheduled to make an appearance. And for the main attraction, Wilbur Wright had agreed (for $15,000) to launch the *Flyer* onto the uncertain winds above the river.

He made the long and narrow Governors Island his base of operations. The Statue of Liberty stood a mile to the west on Bedloe's Island. Wilbur could make his flight anytime he deemed the winds favorable. He had only to send up a signal flag to let crowds and residents along the river know his intentions. A half million people massed along the Brooklyn shore on September 29 when the catapult weight dropped, launching Wilbur lightly into the air. Wilbur circled the island once to furious applause, then climbed to two hundred feet and headed north. At that moment, the *Lusitania* had drawn abreast the Statue of Liberty. When the captain was told that the *Flyer* was in the air, he slowed the engines and called his two thousand passengers onto the decks. They arrived to see a man in a flying machine swooping down in a slow arc around the statue's waist. Then Wilbur tilted the *Flyer* and circled under the upraised torch before gliding once more around the metal drapery at the statue's waist. As Wilbur headed back toward Governors Island, he passed over the *Lusitania* and gazed down at the screaming throng. The captain leaned on the foghorn and a salutatory bellow rose up around Wilbur.

On October 4, Wilbur went up again, and this time he sailed south toward battleships anchored in the harbor. He flew over the British cruisers the *Drake* and the *Argyll* and then shot across the bow of the American *Mississippi*. When reporters asked the *Mississippi*'s captain, William Simms, about the *Flyer*'s military potential, Simms replied that "the aviator's chance of dropping anything on a battleship would be small."

On December 17, 2003, a crowd of around forty thousand gathered on Kill Devil Hill to watch pilot Kevin Kochersberger celebrate the one hundredth anniversary of human flight with a reenactment of the first ascent. The plan to synchronize exactly with Orville Wright's short 10:35 A.M. flight was scratched due to rain. Instead, the US commander in chief, who had flown in on Air Force One, stood up and strung together platitudes and empty phrases. "The United States will always be the first in flight," he concluded. Polite applause followed. The chief executive did not remind the crowd of President Taft's desire to see the airplane used for the good of all nations, and not for war. Instead he listed the aeronautical advances of the past century, including space flight and supersonic speed. He did not mention the *Columbia* disaster ten months earlier, or the planes that had flown into the Twin Towers, or the thousands of American smart bombs that had missed their targets in Iraq. Progress, we are to believe, moves only in one direction, and in one dimension.

Around 2 P.M., Kochersberger's crew, dressed in period hats and black suits, rolled their replica of the *Flyer* out onto a stretch of sand beneath Kill Devil Hill. Two men cranked the propellers, and the biplane, with its forty-foot-long cloth wings, started off. It lurched a few inches into the air, then splashed down in a puddle a foot past the end of the rail. Commentators read into this failure a story of how truly spectacular the Wright flight must have been. But we might also read it as a parable about how little distance, morally speaking, our technology has actually traveled.

Walter Benjamin combined the Marxism of the Frankfurt School and the Kabbalist mysticism of Gershom Scholem to arrive at a singular theory of history whereby the plodding, linear flow of *secular time* could at any moment be derailed and turned into a *messianic fullness of time,* wherein our alienation from nature, from language, from our labor, from one another, would be instantly resolved. Revolution, for Benjamin, meant a transformation of the idea of historical, technological progress into a "now-time," an eternal present where the question of progress makes no sense. For Benjamin, true progress meant an escape *from* history. In this context, the airplane became one of Benjamin's "dialectical images." That is to say, it stood for the German Messerschmitt Me 262 fighter jets that were strafing London, and also for Leonardo's ornithopter, which the inventor had designed to fetch snow from the Alps to be scattered over the summer streets of Florence. One brings relief; the other death. But, said Benjamin, the innocence of Leonardo's invention still lurks within the image of the fighter jet, just as we can still hear echoes of the word *ornithopter* in the terrifying phrase *helicopter gunship.* Benjamin's faith was such that, like Henry Adams, he felt certain that once the savage evidence was in, the world would see how the bombers had betrayed Leonardo's dream. The world would see what a sham the century of flight had become. That realization would mark the true moment of revolution.

THE NEW CREATIONISM

Paddling my canoe along the Kentucky River last fall, I passed beneath hundred-foot-high limestone palisades, following a great blue heron as he too, in short intervals of flight, made his way upriver. I suspected he was heading toward an impressive rookery built in the crown of a dying sycamore that leaned out over the river about a mile upstream. The heron stopped often to preen on deadfalls near the banks, then folded his head and neck into a tight *S* shape and climbed back into the air. At times the heron would wade into the shallows, spear a small silverfish, and then swallow it whole with one quick shiver of his throat. He attacked his prey so fast that his head looked like an arrow shot from his body and tethered to it by that long unspooling neck. I read somewhere that a great blue heron cannot see its reflection in the water. Surely this is an evolutionary adaptation, a way for a fishing bird to better see fish.

I was thinking about blue herons and evolution together because I had been reading Jerry A. Coyne's book *Why Evolution Is True*, which depicts, in four illustrations, the evolution of the

225-million-year-old dinosaur *Coelophysis bauri* into *Compsognathus longipes* of the Late Jurassic, then *Jeholornis prima* from the Lower Cretaceous, and finally *Ardea herodias*, the modern great blue heron. Nineteenth-century paleontologists were the first to notice the similarities in the skeletons of birds and some dinosaurs. Darwin himself knew of the 145-million-year-old fossil *Archaeopteryx lithographica*, a famous transitional form (part bird, part reptile), discovered in 1860 in a German limestone quarry not unlike the gorge I had been paddling through that fall day. In the 1990s, many more "feathered dinosaurs" were discovered in lake sediments throughout China. Like the modern heron, these creatures had an opposable toe for perching. As the fossils get younger (closer to us in time), the reptile tail shrinks and a larger breastbone that could have supported wings and flight begins to appear. According to Coyne, the early transitional birds would have either glided down from trees, like flying squirrels today, or used their wings for propulsion while running, like the contemporary chukar partridge, until they eventually—it must have been quite a shock—took flight.

If I had kept paddling up the Kentucky River, I would have eventually reached the Cumberland Plateau of central Appalachia. John Muir, in his only book about the eastern United States, said that the plateau's oaks were the most beautiful he had ever seen and that its rock shelters were the "most heavenly places" he had ever dropped his pack. Today there are still many such idyllic places throughout the broadleaf forest of eastern Kentucky, but the black-and-gray scar of mountaintop-removal strip mining has annihilated more than five hundred of its mountains, has buried thousands of miles of headwater streams, and is hastening the rise of atmospheric carbon dioxide—a main cause of climate change. What is the connection between coal and evolution? Just this: I believe that a great deal of the current environmental crises can be blamed on our particularly

American and almost willful misunderstanding of Darwin's remarkable theory.

In his introduction to *Why Evolution Is True,* Coyne ponders why, in the face of incontrovertible evidence, 60 percent of Americans still say they do not believe in the theory of evolution. I contend that a fundamental reason—one that has great consequences for both our spiritual and our ecological well-being—is that the religious movement known as creationism ignores one profound fact of life: the entire chorus of life, more than 10 million species, share one common ancestor that first appeared on earth 3.5 billion years ago. For thousands of millions of years, that singular substance took the form of free-floating bacteria, until two billion years ago when they began to form communities, fortresses held together by thin membranes. Then some of the bacteria transformed into oxygen-absorbing mitochondria, and a command center, the nucleus, took shape. The cell was born. Then cells took up residence inside larger organisms, which in turn developed their own protective membranes—shells, flesh, exoskeletons. What followed was the period, from 570 to 530 million years ago, that paleontologists call the Cambrian explosion. Bivalved brachiopods, whose outlines I still see pressed into the limestone banks of this river, emerged, along with the trilobite, bearing a compound eye, and the echinoderms, ancestors to the modern sea urchin and starfish. The marine plants and animals climbed the banks and shores to colonize the terrestrial world. Reptiles turned into dinosaurs and dinosaurs turned into birds. Then whales, porpoises, and primates started swimming and walking around with much larger brains than any species that had come before. At some point, roughly 10 million years ago, an organism that we would recognize in the mirror— evolutionary biologists call her Mitochondrial Eve—walked across the African savanna, plucked the quill from a vulture, and wrote down the story of her origins.

Of course, scientists have been redacting that story ever since, but today the genetic and fossil evidence tells us this: every one of the 10 million species on the planet still retains the same mitochondrial DNA of our common ancestor. This evidence may be the strongest argument for why evolution is *fact*, not theory; or, to use Coyne's words, for why evolution is true. To understand this most basic truth is to realize that human beings are literally, genetically *kin* to all other living creatures. And this kinship seems to me the most sublime and hopeful idea any prophet or philosopher could have ever conjured. It gives us a *reason*, beyond the difficult hope of altruism, to follow the Golden Rule: to treat others—all others—as we wish to be treated, because they are our brothers and sisters, cousins and second cousins.

But this is not how many religious people view the matter. Ever since Darwin published *On the Origin of Species* in 1859, Christians in particular, and American Christians even more particularly, have shuddered at the thought that humans "descended from monkeys." They find it an insult to their intelligence, an affront to the belief that they were created, as the Book of Genesis says, in the image of God. But if all life derived from one substance, why not call that substance God? Why not say that *all* life was created in the image of God?

Actually, I think I will, because what we're really dealing with here is that perennial philosophical problem of the one and the many. Is life made up of one common substance or is it completely heterogeneous, and if the latter, does anything hold all that heterogeneity together? This question haunted the pre-Socratic philosophers. Thales said that all matter is made of water; Heraclitus said fire. And it didn't get settled, at least to my thinking, until when in 1677 Spinoza published his *Ethics*, in which he posits that because God is infinite, the entire universe is comprised of one holy substance that functions as a whole. And because God is infinite, there can be nothing *outside* of God. Spinoza's God is not some other, some creator standing apart from the creation; Spinoza's God *is* the creation. Whenever he invoked the deity, Spinoza always referred to *deus sive natura*—God-or-nature. Nature was at once *natura naturans,* the unique creator, and *natura naturata,* the unique creation. Furthermore, being infinite, God-or-nature possesses limitless "attributes." Because nothing exists outside God-or-nature, that first substance must have been self-created and must continue the act of self-creation by improvising on new attributes—what scientists call species. We might say that all of God-or-nature's improvisations, its adaptations, are the evolutionary work of one self-creating whole.

Spinoza leads us to a compelling conclusion: the surest and closest path to God leads not through the dark night of the soul but rather through the sun-inspired diversity of the natural world. As I paddled along the Kentucky River on that Indian summer day, I felt a strong sense that I was paddling through the aqueous elements out of which all life emerged. The last wildflowers were blooming along the bank, and as I followed the blue heron, I experienced what I think Spinoza meant when he said, "The greatest good is the union that the mind has with the whole of nature."

Which brings me to my point: The true miracle is the world as we find it. A Mediterranean wanderer once even called it the kingdom of God. The great mistake of creationism is that, in schools all across the country, it has tried to teach religion as biology when in fact we should embark on a much more inspiring mission—*to teach biology as religion.*

Creationist thinking sees the world as it wants the world to be, but not as it is. It wants to believe that only humans were created in the likeness of God, separate from all other species. Neither the fossil record nor our standard four-letter DNA code supports this creation story. Aside from it being essentially unsubstantiated, the creationist view strikes me as an extraordinary failure of the imagination. Can we not possibly imagine God as any greater than . . . us? If not, then it's no wonder we treat the rest of creation as nothing more than a "natural resource" to be cut down, mined, polluted, and destroyed.

Creationists all seem obsessed with finding atop Mount Ararat some remnant of Noah's Ark; they write books justifying the ark's historical veracity, right down to discussions of how Noah dealt with the tricky issue of waste management. Yet never have I seen the argument to prove the existence of the ark extended to the logical concern that right now, because of human pressures, the very species that Noah supposedly saved are going extinct at a rate of one per hour. Harvard biologist E. O. Wilson predicts that we could lose *half* of all species by the end of this century.

Why is there no conservation imperative in the creationist movement? Why do these believers want so badly to prove the divine *creation* of the world but have nothing to say about its preservation? Why is their love for the Creator so detached from their concern for the creation? Why are they not awestruck, as was Job, when the voice in the whirlwind details the astonishing diversity of this rare planet?

Answers have been proffered, of course. Perhaps the most common one points to the Book of Genesis, where Yahweh gave man "dominion" over the world. I have often heard strip miners cite the "dominion" passage as their rationale for tearing apart the mountains of Appalachia. But this is nothing more than a flimsy justification for desecrating the creation. It is a violation of the laws of nature and therefore a violation of the law of the Creator, the law of divine providence. According to the United Nations' Millennium Ecosystem Assessment, human beings have now degraded 60 percent of all "ecosystem services" to unsustainable levels. In the great "satanic mills" that poet William

Blake brooded over, we are quite literally setting the world on fire. It isn't simply unsustainable—it is a sacrilege. To begin to see the natural world as a sacred place, an unroofed church, is the first way—and perhaps the only way—to convince the majority of Americans that we must stop destroying it. This pastoral impulse can be traced back to Thomas Jefferson's plea for Americans to resist a manufacturing economy because "those who labour in the earth are the chosen people of God, if ever he had a chosen people, whose breasts he has made his peculiar deposit for substantial and genuine virtue." I propose therefore a new creationism, one that really does look to nature as a scripture wherein we can read miracle after miracle: the awesome spectacle of a flying squirrel gliding through a forest's understory; the African tailor bird, which sews together two leaves for its nest with a long piece of grass; the ongoing creation and regeneration of topsoil. This new creationism would hinge on two principles—one scientific, the other religious:

1. All of life was born from one substance, and therefore all of creation is linked by a kinship.
2. That original substance was God.

I know some of my biologist friends will shudder at this second principle, but unlike the teaching of religion as biology, the teaching of biology as religion does not violate any scientific method; it simply imbues matter with spirit and thus overcomes a terrible dualism that has always lingered at the heart of fundamental Christianity, a dualism that has allowed for much abuse of the natural world. The creationists, after all, got the *word* right; they simply have been looking at the creation through the wrong end of the telescope. To understand the natural world as a divine scripture is to imbue the creation with the holy and to begin treating it as such.

There is, in fact, a biblical precedent for this, and it can be found in a gospel that many New Testament scholars now believe is older than Matthew, Mark, Luke, or John.[1] At the beginning of the Gospel of Thomas, Jesus's followers ask him about their great preoccupation, the kingdom of God. Jesus replies, "If your leaders say to you, 'Look, the kingdom is in heaven,' then the birds of heaven will

---

[1] There are many convincing reasons why the Gospel of Thomas is older than Mark's Gospel. For starters, Thomas does not mention the destruction of the Second Temple. It seems unlikely that any Jewish writer would have ignored such a disastrous turn of events if he or she had lived through it, which suggests that Thomas was composed before 72 CE. Helmut Koester of the Harvard Divinity School has also noted that Thomas must have come from an early group that was still appealing to the authority of the men who would become the Pillars of Jerusalem—Peter, James, and John. In Thomas 12, the "followers" say to Jesus, "We know that you are going to leave us. Who will be our leader?" Jesus said to them, "No matter where you are, you are to go to James the Just, for whose sake heaven and earth came into being." Since James died in 62 CE, that would date Thomas's gospel well before Mark's. It is also worth noting here that in Thomas, Jesus has only followers, not the symbolic "twelve disciples" later revered by Matthew and Luke as symbolic counterparts to the twelve tribes of Israel. That, along with the fact that, in Thomas, Jesus is never called "Christ" or "Lord" or the "Son of God," suggests that those titles came later and were applied by the Pauline communities to whom the significance of Jesus's death had overshadowed and nearly replaced the message of his teachings. If Jesus had been the Messiah, if he had performed the miracles attributed to him by Luke, he certainly would have attracted some attention. He lived, after all, very close to large Roman cities like Tiberias and Sepphoris. But Jesus never did draw much attention. If he had, *some* Roman historian would have certainly taken notice. None did, which leads one to suspect that while Jesus may have had the shaman-like powers to exorcise psychic demons in people, he did not routinely walk on water and raise the dead. On the contrary, the Roman historian Tacitus wrote of the time when Jesus would have been wandering and teaching: *Sub Tiberio quies*—"Under Tiberius, nothing happened." But the most substantial evidence for the early composition of Thomas lies in the sayings themselves as compared to the synoptic Gospels. Stephen J. Patterson has shown that Thomas only resembles Matthew and Luke when all three Gospels are independently using an earlier source—one now known as Q. When there are similar sayings in Thomas and the synoptic Gospels that don't rely on Q, the wording of the sayings differs too widely to suggest Thomas's dependence on the other Gospels. In addition, Thomas almost never orders his sayings in the same sequence as Matthew, Mark, and Luke, which he certainly would have done had they been his sources. Perhaps the best argument for Thomas as the earliest account of Jesus's teachings is the way he simply lets them stand on their own, without adding an interpretation that would align Jesus with the theological biases of later writers. One might suppose that the compilers of Thomas and Q presumably *knew* the context of the sayings, and saw no reason to replicate it, nor did they try to distort it to fit their own theological biases.

precede you. If they say to you, 'It is in the sea,' then the fish will precede you. Rather, the kingdom is inside you and it is outside you." Here Jesus is obviously mocking the traditional understanding of a kingdom on high. And the futile gesture of looking "in the sea" for the kingdom of God reminds me of a Persian parable in which a single fish spends its entire existence searching for the ocean. Only when a trawler's net finally catches the fish does it look down at the ocean and realize it had been swimming there its whole life. We make the same mistake, Jesus is telling his followers in the Gospel of Thomas. The only thing that prevents us from seeing the actual, immediate world as the kingdom of God is our own blindness to it, our own obtuse insistence that it must lie somewhere else. Like the rooms in our own homes, the familiar seems so common to us that we fail to see it at all, and we certainly fail to see it as anything extraordinary. This, essentially, is the genius of Thomas's itinerant Jesus: he has, in his own words, cast a new light on the world so that the most common occurrences—seeds sprouting in the dark ground, we know not why—become evidence that the natural world is the immanent kingdom of God. In Thomas's Gospel, Jesus performs no miracles because, presumably, the creation itself is the one true miracle, could we only see it as such. But we don't, and so even in the penultimate saying of Thomas's Gospel, the fishermen following Jesus seem to have learned nothing:

> His followers said to him, "When will the kingdom come?"
> "It will not come by watching for it. It will not be said, 'Look, here it is,' or 'Look, there it is.' Rather, the father's kingdom is spread out upon the earth, and people do not see it."

Of course, in Luke 17:20–21, Jesus makes a similar claim about the *basileia tou theo*. But scholars have puzzled over whether Luke's Greek should be translated as "the kingdom of God is within you" or "the kingdom of God is in your midst." Thomas leaves no doubt when he records Jesus as saying that "the kingdom is inside you and it is outside you." This collapses and separates out both translations of Luke's Greek into two more lucid and beautiful ideas. The first is revealed when, "Jesus said, 'Know what is in front of your face, and what is hidden from you will be disclosed to you. For there is nothing hidden that will not be revealed.'" He demands that his followers actually *pay attention* to the variegated beauty of the natural world. He is, in effect, telling them to stop trying to be theologians or eschatologists and instead become . . . *biologists.* More to the point, he is telling them to see the laws of God in the laws of nature. Then "what is hidden"—God's law—will be revealed in what is "disclosed"—the law of nature. In Thomas's Gospel, Jesus follows up this idea with a powerful corollary—that there is a kingdom within us that is a reflection of the kingdom spread out before us. It is as if the tips of two triangles meet at one point and when they touch, both are transformed by the other. Biology becomes an interior, spiritual enterprise.

Or to shift metaphors, I sometimes imagine this point as the surface of a two-way mirror, an image inspired by Coleman Banks's limpid translation of Fariduddin Attar's twelfth-century epic poem *Manteq at-Tair—The Conference of the Birds.* The poem is an allegory in which the world's birds gather to search for their king, called the Simurgh. The journey, which will take them across "the seven valleys of the Way," is fraught with hazards, and when the flock finally reaches the last valley, it has been thinned to only thirty (*si-*) birds (*-murgh*). This is the pun on which the poem depends, because when the thirty birds reach the chamber of the Simurgh, they enter a kind of trance:

> *and in each other's faces they saw*
> *the inner world. They did not know*
> *if they were still themselves,*
> *or if they had become God.*

At last, in a deep state of contemplation,
they knew they were the Simurgh,
and that the Simurgh was the thirty birds.

They saw both as one and the same being.
No experience can equal that experience.

What the birds finally come to understand is that the creation is an extension, a manifestation of the Creator. In this realization, the entire history of dualistic Western logic, reaching back to the Tree of the Knowledge of Good and Evil, is vanquished. The knowledge of divine emanation replaces the postlapsarian knowledge of separation from God. In the "outer" world of each other's faces the birds see the "inner" world of their God. And that inner world has shown forth a light that infuses the physical with the spiritual, that reveals the manifest world as the kingdom of God. Such a realization leads the birds into a deeper state of mediation:

and after a little they asked the Simurgh,
without using language, to reveal the mystery
of the unity and the multiplicity of beings.

Without speaking, the answer came, "This majesty
is a mirror. If you approach as thirty birds,
that's what you will find. Forty or fifty
birds would come and see forty and fifty.

And although you are now completely changed,
you see yourselves as you were before.

You did well to be astounded and impatient
and doubting and full of wonder.

Lose yourselves in me joyfully,
and you will find yourselves."

The Simurgh is telling the birds the same thing Jesus is telling his followers in Thomas's Gospel: We in our multiplicity still harbor the divine presence of the original one, the source and the reconciliation of all being. When we look in the mirror, we must see both; we must see ourselves as we are, and we must see that we are still imbued with what Jesus calls the "father's light" in this crucial passage:

> Jesus said, "Images are visible to people, but the light within them is hidden in the image of the father's light. He will be disclosed, but his image is hidden by his light."
> Jesus said, "When you see your likeness, you are happy. But when you see your images that came into being before you and that neither die nor become visible, how much you will bear!"

Again, Jesus is telling his followers what the Simurgh tells the birds— the one (light) still exists in the presence of the many (images), but it is simultaneously a revealing and a concealing presence that can be known only through a more-than-rational knowledge that by its nature escapes language and logic. This intuitive knowledge has often gone by the name *gnosis*, and passages like the one above have often led commentators to insert the adjective *gnostic* in front of the title the Gospel of Thomas. Many versions of Christian gnosticism circulated in the centuries that followed the life of Jesus, but to me, gnosticism's central tenet is that we all carry within us that original light (a divine spark, it is sometimes called) of the Creator. But that light cannot be known rationally through the five senses, and so a new way of knowing—gnosis—is required. Through such gnosis, we understand that the eternal one is constantly passing through the earth's temporal forms, its millions of species. But because that force cannot be contained within an image, Jesus falls back on the paradoxical idea of an *imageless image of light*—the face we had before we were born. Like a Zen koan, this seemingly contradictory idea jams our rational thought processes and throws us over into the contemplative realm of gnosis. And it is there that we might recognize, just as the birds do when staring at their own images, that the multifarious images of our individual selves are still illuminated by the original light of the one—that they are one and the same because the creation is an emanation of the Creator, and therefore one cannot be separated from the other.

Thus my second principle of the new creationism—the original substance of life, and of the universe, can be called God—is not science but a gnosis. Yet it cannot contradict evolution or any other scientific fact because the physical laws are also the laws of the Creator: *deus sive natura,* God-or-nature. But whether we are talking about gnostic intuitions or scientific observation, our subject remains the kingdom of God, and what I find so fascinating and inspiring about Jesus's message in the Gospel of Thomas is the way in which he reconciles a spiritual gnosis with a biological view of nature. In fact, I would claim that the sayings in Thomas represent a truly ecological gospel because, while we can accept the original imageless image as a source of gnostic contemplation, we can also ground that idea in contemporary evolutionary biology. Consider this saying, for example, which can be read as simply a description of the first cell's division, one that no evolutionary biologist would contradict: "Jesus said, 'On the day when you were one, you became two. But when you become two, what will you do?'" This is almost the same question that Attar's birds ask the Simurgh about the one and the many. Perhaps it has been such a persistent question in Western philosophy because it implies that some sense of unity was severed and we were cast adrift on a chaotic, possibly random sea of multiplicity. But in this saying, Jesus seems to understand the question as both theological and biological. Twenty-one hundred years later, evolutionary biologists have answered their side of it by proving that the entire chorus of life shares one common ancestor, and so we are all kin to one another. That implies, to state what is obvious but too often ignored, that since all species on earth are kin, we should *act* like it. And *that,* I think, is the answer to Jesus's question: When we realize that the one has split into two, we should also understand that the two are still bound together—biologically, theologically, and morally—because they are descended from the one. In a later saying, Jesus implies that when we achieve this level of reconciliation, something miraculous will happen: "Jesus said, 'When you make the two into one, you will become children of humanity,' and when you say, 'Mountain, move from here,' it will move." Just as life and death are always a closed loop feeding into one another, so the many feed back into the one. Only this time, what unifies them is not only a biological understanding of genetic kinship but also a spiritual epiphany that the natural world is a kingdom of God.

SPEAK AND BEAR WITNESS

I did not go to eastern Kentucky ten years ago looking to get mauled by bulldozers or pummeled by rocks that rain from the sky when mountains are blown apart. In the beginning, I went to the broad-leaf forests of central Appalachia—the most biologically diverse ecosystems in North America—to write poetry. More specifically, I would drive from my home in Lexington to Robinson Forest, a fifteen-thousand-acre woodland in the eastern part of the state. There I would spend days and weeks living in a chestnut cabin, meandering along Kentucky's cleanest streams and up some of its steepest slopes. It was John Clare, I believe, who said he didn't write his poems but simply found them lying in the fields. Wandering the mountains and streams of Robinson Forest, I amused myself by thinking that poems would come just as easily to me. And why not? I had retreated into just about the deepest pastoral seclusion one can find in the state of Kentucky. In another culture, in another time, these magnificent oaks might have constituted a goddess's sacred grove. Certainly some semblance of the muse had to be hovering over my shoulder.

I knew, of course, there was a terrible machine rumbling at the outskirts of this woodland paradise. When I was a kid, my great-grandparents owned a clothing store in the nearest town, Hazard, and when we drove down to visit them, I could see along the roadside the great gashes that bulldozers had cut into the mountains. I knew what strip mining was, and I knew it was thought to be as inevitable to eastern Kentucky as poverty and kudzu. Few people questioned it, and as I said, I hadn't gone to Robinson Forest looking to cause trouble, or to get into any. Just the opposite, in fact. I was hoping that the inscrutable spirits of the natural world might still my own restless, urban nature. Like transcendentalists of the nineteenth century, I believed—and still believe—in the power of the great god Pan. And if a hot July afternoon found me lying flat on my back in a shallow stream, then that was all the baptism I needed.

All of that changed in 2002. While staying in Robinson Forest that summer, I spent some time with a group of wildlife biologists who were reintroducing an elk herd into eastern Kentucky. But as I would come to learn, these were not the eastern elk that had been hunted to extinction in 1867. These were Rocky Mountain elk, shipped in from Colorado, and because of that, the unnatural landscape of a strip mine looked much more native to them than the dense forest preferred by the original eastern elk. Which is to say, I ended up spending far more time wandering around strip jobs than I ever thought I would. But by then, no one really used the term *strip mining* anymore. It seemed like everyone, particularly environmentalists, had started to call the practice mountaintop removal. And from what I was beginning to see, the new label was far more accurate, even if it sounded misleadingly clinical. This wasn't the auger mining of my childhood, when only the sides of a mountain were cut away. Now coal operators were mixing ammonium nitrate and fuel oil together to literally blast to pieces the entire summit of a mountain, and then they dumped everything that wasn't coal into the streams and rivers below.

One day after tracking a young elk herd with the wildlife biologists, I climbed to the top of the fire tower in Robinson Forest. I had done this many times before to watch the sun set and the fog move in. But for some reason, on that day it struck me that Robinson Forest was an island of life surrounded by the deadest, most barren landscapes east of the Mojave Desert. Standing at the top of the fire tower, I suddenly understood that I could no longer write about the untrammeled beauty of Robinson Forest without also writing about the forces at work to destroy it.

That has become a kind of creation story for me. Any success I have had as an "environmental writer" (a term I don't particularly like) came because of what I experienced standing at the top of the fire tower and what I did after I climbed down. Specifically, I went to the Office of Natural Resources in Frankfort, Kentucky, and started perusing permits for mountaintop-removal jobs. The bound permits were all about fifteen inches thick and written in a dense, impenetrable language. I could make little of it. All I knew—and I knew this only intuitively—was that I had to write something about the perils of mountaintop removal. But I wasn't a mining engineer, I wasn't a biologist, I wasn't a lawyer, I wasn't a regulator, I wasn't a legislator, I wasn't a hydrologist, I wasn't an activist. I wasn't even a journalist, unless you count the music reviews I wrote for my college newspaper back in the late eighties. In short, I possessed none of the expertise that seemed necessary to understanding the complexities of MTR. But then, haplessly flipping through one permit, I pulled out a map. It showed, with a perforated line, the original contour of a mountain. Then, with two flat lines, it showed what the peak would look like after coal operators lopped off its top. In the space between the flat lines and the jagged, perforated lines were two words in capital letters: LOST MOUNTAIN. At last, here was something I did know how to do—perceive irony. If the coal operators had their way, they would decapitate Lost Mountain, and it would be, well, lost. Not lost in the sense that it couldn't be found, but lost in the sense that it could never be recovered. It would be rendered irretrievable, destroyed, killed. Sitting alone among those sagging shelves of permits, I suddenly knew that I would write a book called *Lost Mountain*.

Beyond my attenuated sense of irony, I thought I had two more things going for me. I was a pretty good observer of detail—I had learned that from my mentor, Guy Davenport—and I could tell, at least in writing, a decent story. Given that I could claim no expertise on the subject of strip mining, I decided I would simply try to tell, through direct observation, the story of one mountain. I would climb it at least once a month for a year, and I would recount, firsthand, the story of its destruction. Having seen the permit map, I knew how the story would end. It would end badly. But I didn't know—and due to the steep contours of the mountains and the secrecy of the coal industry hardly anyone else knew—what happened between the felling of the first tree and the rooting out of the last block of coal. So I went to see.

Though I worked hard to learn from journalists I admired, I didn't want to write a journalistic account exactly. Instead I tried to approach Lost Mountain the way I had first entered Robinson Forest: I wanted to see the flora and fauna with the eye of an amateur naturalist and the disposition of a Romantic poet. I wanted to create a portrait of Lost Mountain that might stir certain feelings for the place, a sense of affinity that went beyond some abstract idea that preserving abstract "nature" is a good thing to do. Even though I knew it was too late for Lost Mountain, I wanted to show, as clearly as I could, what was being destroyed and why other Appalachian mountains should be preserved.

But to create such a portrait of Lost Mountain, I obviously had to see it up close, and that meant I had to trespass. (A few years later, I heard the president of the Kentucky Coal Association tell a group of students that I had set a terrible moral example for them.) I had to sneak past the mine gates or up the back of the mountain. I had to dodge the omnipresent white pickup trucks that signified mine foremen or supervisors. And I had to try not to get hit by the detonated debris that the industry rather benignly calls "flyrock." I suppose one could call this the work of an investigative reporter, but that's not really how it felt. Instead, I understood myself to be inscribing a tombstone, as Edward Abbey said of his book *Desert Solitaire*, and I wanted it to be a grave one indeed, a weight that, in Abbey's words, could be thrown "at something big and glassy."

At the beginning, I took a lot of field notes, sketching the tracks of deer, raccoons, turkeys, and foxes. I explored the rich ecological communities that lived in and around the capstones of Lost Mountain. I watched and listened to ovenbirds and wood thrushes flitting through the understory of the mountain's oak–hickory canopy. Once, by mistake, I even picked up a copperhead—thankfully a cold and lethargic one. I often did these things on the back side of the mountain, where the headwaters of Lost Creek come alive. One spring day, I was standing in deep, damp shade, writing the words *spotted trillium* in my notebook, when an explosion shook the entire mountain. I fell, startled, into Lost Creek. And that, as much as anything, represented the sorry contradiction I wanted to capture—North America's most biologically diverse ecosystem being blown asunder by the forces that power our culture of acquisitive convenience.

I eventually got to know Lost Mountain so well that I could be standing, unnoticed, about thirty feet from a bulldozer that was busy scraping away one of its sandstone spurs. Hiding behind a large chestnut oak, the last one left before the ridge side plunged into a cratered pit, I could make out the tattoos on the driver's arm. And usually, at the end of the day, after the dozer had shut down and the strip miners were gone, I would sit on the large capstone at the top of Lost Mountain and take it all in. The Carolina wrens and red-eyed vireos would start singing again as I sat in the quiet of late afternoon and tried to get my head around what I was seeing. John Keats once said that the sign of a good mind is that it can hold two opposing thoughts at once. But I could never do that up on Lost Mountain. I couldn't let the industrial thought that was destroying this place sit beside the ecological thought that said the mountain knows what it's doing and had been doing it for a few billion years before someone with opposable thumbs got around to inventing a D-11 dozer. I decided that more important than holding in mind two irreconcilable thoughts was seizing on one of those thoughts and turning it into words, into action. In the end, I can say that my experience on Lost Mountain turned me into a Jamesian prag-matist—someone who believes a thought isn't really *worth* having unless it can be converted into an act of conscience.

Is writing such an act? I think it can be. I wouldn't call what I wrote about Lost Mountain a strict act of advocacy or activism any more than I would call it a strict act of journalism. But seventy years ago, in "The Land Ethic," which is to my thinking the most important piece of twentieth-century American nonfiction, Aldo Leopold set down the guiding principles for how we might resign our roles as conquerors of the natural world and instead become members of a land community: "A thing is right when it tends to preserve the integrity, stability and beauty of the biotic community. It is wrong when it tends otherwise." This clear and profound dis-tinction between right and wrong, between the ethical and the un-ethical, can carry us quite far when it comes to thinking about acts of conscience (what is mountaintop removal if not the ultimate act of *dis*integration, *in*stability, and ugliness). And any writing about the land and its people that proceeds from Leopold's premise will be such an act, and it will likely inspire other acts that take many other forms beyond writing.

One of the great embodiments of such a writerly act of conscience took place eighty years ago, not far from Lost Mountain. In 1931 coal industry gun thugs surrounded the house of a union organizer named Sam Reece, hoping to ambush him. They waited all night. Reece never came home, but inside the house, his wife, Florence, tore a page down from a wall calendar, and huddled on the floor with her children, she wrote the twentieth century's most famous union song, "Which Side Are You On?" Written to the tune of the traditional ballad "Lay the Lily Low," the song takes on the brutal Harlan County sheriff J. H. Blair and the violent men he deputized to kill union miners. The last three verses go like this:

> *They say in Harlan County,*
> *There are no neutrals there.*
> *You'll either be a union man,*
> *Or a thug for J. H. Blair.*
> *Oh, workers can you stand it?*
> *Oh, tell me how you can.*
> *Will you be a lousy scab,*
> *Or will you be a man?*
> *Don't scab for the bosses,*
> *Don't listen to their lies.*
> *Us poor folks haven't got a chance,*
> *Unless we organize.*

Then comes the chorus, which simply repeats the question of the title over and over: "Which side are you on, boys, which side are you on?" I've sung that anthem at many rallies, often with verses updated to reflect the contemporary struggles of the coalfields. One of the song's many virtues is clarity. It says that one side has the power and one side does not. And unfortunately, the latter is the side of conscience. So the only way to take hold of the power wielded by the coal operators is to act—to act together, to act on principle, and to act in public.

Thus the composing of "Which Side Are You On?" was a solitary act that has inspired great acts of solidarity. Writing *is* a solitary act—but it's only the first act. What comes next is what really matters. However, honestly, personally, I have never been all that comfortable with the second act. I'm a solitary person by nature and not much of a joiner. Yet still I've come to see the nonfiction writer's solitary act as important to the greater cause of decreasing cruelty and increasing sympathy. In that service, nonfiction writers can perform two fundamental tasks that are unavailable to the writers of fiction. Like Florence Reece, we can bear witness and we can call for change—for an end to injustices.

It is precisely on this subject of bearing witness that I find John D'Agata's recent writing about the genre of nonfiction so malicious and inept. D'Agata argues that nonfiction must serve the greater good of art, and therefore reality can be altered in the name of art. But to elevate reality to the level of art is one of the fundamental tasks of the nonfiction writer, and to say it cannot be done honestly, as D'Agata claims, displays an astonishing lack of imagination as well as an equally unflattering amount of arrogance and pedantry. But let's put aside the either-or nature of this line of thinking. The real problem here is that such an attitude robs nonfiction of its greatest strength and virtue—its ability to bear witness and the veracity that comes from that act. To admit that one only has a passing interest in representing reality is to forfeit one's moral authority to call that reality into question. That is to say, I have no right to call mountaintop removal an injustice—one in need of a new reality— if I cannot be trusted to depict the travesty of strip mining as it now exists. To play D'Agata's game is to lose the reader's trust, and without that, it seems to me that the nonfiction writer has very little left. Writers of that persuasion can align themselves with Picasso's famous sentiment that art is the lie that tells the truth, but I have no truck with such pretentiousness. The work of the nonfiction writers I most admire is telling a truth that exposes a lie.

This makes the nonfiction writer a close cousin to the documentary filmmaker. The documentarian's images are vitally important, especially to a cause like mountaintop removal, where everyone needs to *see* a mountain being blasted to rubble. But the written word works on the brain in ways very different from, though complementary to, the visual image. If the visual image is more immediate, more visceral, the word provides the reader with the time and the space to linger, cogitate, and wrestle with the implications of what was just said. The reader invests in the work of prose in a way that is often more deliberate and more engaged than with film— which may explain why the brain is most active when reading than at any other time except dreaming.

I've been called a dreamer quite a lot since writing *Lost Mountain*. Only in this context, the term usually means that I'm someone who is used to losing. And that's true. For the environmental writer, losing is simply an occupational hazard. But I believe the appropriate response to Florence Reece's "Which Side Are You On?" is not, "I'm on the side that's going to win," but rather, "I'm on the side of conscience, empathy, and affection."

Because my last name has the same unusual spelling as Florence Reece's (with a *c* instead of an *s*), people sometimes ask if I'm related to her. Unfortunately, I've never been able to prove a family connection, but in any case, that's the side I'm on—the side of Florence and Sam Reece, the side of the mountain, the side of the men and women who are dying because the air and the water around Appalachian strip mines isn't fit to breathe and drink. If that's the losing side, then it simply means there is more work to do, more words to get down. The prospect doesn't depress me. I'm well aware of Aldo Leopold's warning that "one of the penalties of an ecological education is that one lives alone in a world of wounds." It is a world of wounds, but it's all we have, and we are not alone. The solitary act of creative nonfiction writing leads to the second act of solidarity with readers who are willing to bear witness through the writer's words, who are then willing to act.

EIGHT DRAFTS OF A SUICIDE NOTE

1.

To stand in the Tate Gallery's Rothko Room, surrounded by nine massive canvases, all painted in the corpuscular hues of blood and wine, is to find oneself suspended, outside narrative time, outside spatial imagery: in utero, or in a cave.

In each painting, a nebulous portal—black, maroon, or scarlet— hovers against a muted red backdrop. These passageways hang like momentary architecture, thresholds of smoke. Of all Rothko's abstract work, these are the only paintings that we might legitimately say have perspective, depth of field. They hang as a door between two realms: the sayable and the unsayable. Each canvas pulls us toward its opening, pointing beyond. But where? To what?

The murals were originally commissioned as "decorations" (so read the contract) for the Four Seasons Restaurant in Mies van der Rohe's Seagram Building on Park Avenue. Rothko was to deliver "500 to 600 square feet of paintings" for $35,000. Rothko signed on. At first he seemed to take it as a challenge. "I hope to paint something that will ruin the appetite of every son of a bitch who ever eats in that room," he told *Harper's* editor John Fischer. Toward that end he employed a darker palette, "more somber than anything I've tried before." Rothko once admitted to his assistant, Dan Jensen, that perhaps "comedy, ecstasy and loftiness of spirit are what I actually stand for and that I only exploit talk about tragedy and despair." Such an argument could certainly have been made before 1957. Where, after all, is the tragedy in an orange square floating about a purple rectangle against a yellow background? But in the following years, as Rothko's life grew bleaker—emphysema, alcoholism, an irreparable marriage—he sank into real darkness. However inadvertently, the Seagram commission gave him a final language to speak that despair.

After a disastrous dinner visit to the Four Seasons, Rothko told Mies's assistant, a young Philip Johnson, that the uptown bourgeoisie didn't deserve his art. He voided his contract with the Four Seasons and instead sold the nine paintings he had completed to the Tate Gallery in London. These nine paintings arrived at the Tate on February 25, 1970, the day Mark Rothko took his life. This, no doubt, is one reason I have come to think of them as drafts of the suicide note Rothko never actually wrote. Another reason is that suicide—specifically, my father's—is something I was struggling to understand one year in my twenties when I took a hiatus from formal education and moved for a semester to Oxford, England. I paid rent for a tiny room above the garage of a working-class family, and every weekend I took a bus to the Tate Gallery, where I spent hours lost in the massive paintings that Mark Rothko bequeathed to the Tate. Sitting on those benches, staring at those fields of red, I began to realize that Rothko's late paintings might reveal some vital information about my own father's final act.

2.

My father, like his father, was a Baptist minister. He shot himself with a hunting rifle when I was three. My grandfather was a forceful fundamentalist preacher in the Tidewater area of Virginia. My father, apparently with some trepidation, followed him into the ministry. But he was not as successful a preacher as my grandfather, who could overwhelm a congregation with the power of his conviction, and at some point my father began to doubt whether he felt truly called to the ministry at all. Moreover, he began to doubt the strict literalism of my grandfather's version of Christianity. In his own mind, he had not lived up to his father's standard as a minister, and to make matters worse, he felt that he had secretly betrayed his father's faith. My father punished himself with guilt and anxiety. That, compounded by a bipolar disorder, caused him to turn a gun on himself on September 1, 1970.

After my father's death, I labored unconsciously to fill the void he had left, to be so "good" in my grandparents' eyes that I would in some way make them forget their great loss. As a child, I told everyone that I too was going to be a minister and carry on the family legacy. As a teenager I led youth retreats at our church and abstained from all of the usual adolescent seductions. Then gradually, I became infected with the same doubt that had plagued my father. I had done some reading in a textbook on abnormal psychology and discovered that bipolar disease is passed on only to children of the opposite sex. It seemed I had been spared that, but the doubt—followed by guilt—remained and increased. My family's fundamentalism began to feel like a penal system meant, as the poet William Blake put it, "to bind with briars/my joys and desires." It became insufferable, and by the time I reached Oxford, feeling close to some breakdown of my own, I decided that the best way to avoid my father's fate was to abandon my family's religion. To that end, I immersed myself in the writing of Friedrich Nietzsche, convinced that Nietzsche's post-Christian philosophy might help disentangle me from the "mind-forg'd manacles" (Blake again) that I was convinced had doomed my father.

It felt like I was on the right tack. Sitting on the banks of the Thames River, I read Ronald Hayman's biography of Nietzsche. There I learned that Nietzsche's father and grandfather had also been protestant ministers and that his father had died of some brain disease when Friedrich was a boy. The young Nietzsche's response, like mine, had been to embrace piety in an effort to please his grandparents, so much so that his elementary schoolmates mocked him and called him "the little minister." But twenty years later, in his first book, *The Birth of Tragedy,* the little minister began what would be the most sustained attack on the organized church that Western philosophy had ever seen. Reading that book for the first time in my twenties, I felt as if Nietzsche were speaking my deepest doubts back to me in words I could never have found on my own.

In Nietzsche's sweeping claim that art is a healthier metaphysic than religion, I recognized for the first time the trapdoor through which I might escape my own family drama. Rothko's own debt to *The Birth of Tragedy* has been well documented by Dore Ashton and Brian O'Doherty. And according to his biographer, James E. B. Breslin, Rothko made extensive notes toward a commentary he hoped to write on Nietzsche's first book. He must have immediately recognized how Nietzsche's own analysis of the elemental power of music—abstract by definition—provided an analogue to his own intense and imageless art. Nietzsche believed that Socratic rationalism had robbed Greek tragedy, and life itself, of an elemental vitality. "Will it not some day rise once again out of its mystical depths as art?" he wondered. Certainly Rothko wanted his paintings to be an answer in the affirmative.

It's clear from notes Nietzsche was making around 1870 that the twenty-six-year-old professor of philology had already decided on his life's work: he would topple Platonism, pull the gods out of the sky, and reestablish beauty—*appearance*—as a better myth than truth. He began this project in *The Birth of Tragedy* by borrowing from Jules Michelet the distinction between the Apollonian and Dionysian, a distinction he thought went to the very core of Western consciousness. From there he could trace ahead to where it had gone wrong, where it had become Socratic, Christian—*moral.* The book is a breathless, idiosyncratic series of moves, grounded in the rather obscure story of "wise Silenus," whom King Midas hunted down one day because he wanted to know the "best and most desirable of all things for man." Like all oracles, Silenus was reluctant to speak. But when the king refused to let him go, the wise man confessed: "What is best is utterly beyond your reach: not to be born, not to *be,* to be *nothing.*" Here, Silenus stands as the true voice of Dionysus. His message: total annihilation—suicide. And, argued Nietzsche, it was precisely this terrifying answer that gave birth to the true Apollonian culture of the Greeks. Whereas Dionysus stood for chaos, Apollo sculpted that senseless matter into art; he gave it form. And of course it was the Greeks who created Apollo. For life to be bearable at all, the Greeks had to invent a pantheon of gods. Why? Because, wrote Nietzsche, "the gods justify the life of man: they themselves live it—the only satisfactory theodicy! Existence under the bright sunshine of such gods is regarded as desirable in itself." Given this, a Greek or Christian morality that was "hostile to life," that invented a metaphysical realm superior to this life, amounted to a betrayal of our Western birthright. Art, not morality, is "the truly *metaphysical* activity of man," Nietzsche concluded. That is to say, when we stare down the existential reality that the world contains great suffering, we have essentially two choices: We can hope for a better realm, and pray to be rescued into it, or we can find a way to make this world acceptable, inhabitable, meaningful. Philosophy and religion had always represented the first answer; art the second. And according to Nietzsche, those with the courage to accept their fate—to *celebrate* it, *amor fati*—gave birth to Greek tragedy.

The title of Nietzsche's first book comes from his assertion that tragedy was born out of music. The Dionysian chorus came first. Only later did scenes and characters emerge. Nietzsche imagined tragedy evolving in the same way we tend to think of existence coming into being: From a formless force, some great breath, the world of things was called into existence. Music was the force that gave birth to imagery, language, the plastic arts, just as all those arts aspire, in the end, toward music. This, said Nietzsche, was as it should be. Form-giving Apollo showed us how to invent ourselves as individuals—*principium individuationis*—even as he recognized the tragic impermanence of a life Dionysus would eventually rend asunder. But Dionysus could never be denied. It was crucial for Nietzsche that we experience both at once: the Apollonian individual and the Dionysian force that he called "primordial being itself"—"the *one* living being" that erased all distinctions. He chose a metaphor from Schopenhauer to best illustrate this dialectic: Apollonian culture and its *principium individuationis* is but a small boat made from frail bark, tossed by the punishing storms of Dionysian nature. The boat is the "Apollonian world of beauty"; the sea is "the terrible wisdom of Silenus." Together they consummate "the perpetually attained goal of the primal unity, its redemption through mere appearance." In this version of redemption, life isn't a trial to gain admission into an unworldly kingdom of God. This *is* the kingdom; but we must invent it, enact it, ourselves.

To Nietzsche, the unpardonable sin of Socrates and of late Hellenic culture as a whole was that it tried to push our Apollonian character to the point that we abandoned Dionysus. Socrates represented the victory of the rational, or the illusion of reason's victory. At this point, tragedy itself committed suicide in the guise of Euripides. The chorus was pushed to the edge of the stage. Poets had no place in a culture where everything could be explained logically. Dionysus was driven underground. It was no accident, as Nietzsche saw it, that the death of tragedy happened simultaneously with the birth of morality, philosophy, Christianity. Nietzsche's ambition, and to some extent his success, was to announce the death of Socrates and the rebirth of Dionysus—the death of Christianity and the resurrection of art. If philosophy from Socrates forward had been an arduous attempt to abandon Plato's famous cave, Nietzsche was ready to lead everyone right back down into that dark theater of ritual and art.

And so was Mark Rothko.

3.

There are few photographs where Rothko appears at ease. At times he admits a smile in the company of his cat, or his children (never with his wife, Mell). But for the most part, Rothko looks deeply uncomfortable in his own skin. His body weighed him down. Only through painting did he ever seem to achieve levity, loftiness. There is, though, one often-reproduced photograph by Hans Namuth in which Rothko does appear content. He is sitting in a green, wooden deck chair before a six-by-eight canvas, contemplating a maroon square against a red, rectangular background. He is smoking a cigarette (a Lark!). Though the photo is taken from behind, the slouch of Rothko's frame and the tilt of his head suggest satisfaction with his work, even with himself.

Many writers have made the connection between Rothko's admiration for Matisse's *Red Studio* and what seemed like a literal attempt to create that space with the red murals that would eventually become the Rothko Room at the Tate. Dore Ashton described a visit in 1959 to Rothko's "cavernous studio with its deep-dyed red floor."

Versions of the Seagram murals surrounded her. The room was "dim as a cathedral" or an ancient library. Clearly this was not the bourgeois interior of Matisse's painting. Now, when I look at the Namuth photograph of Rothko in his wooden chair, surrounded by these walls of intense dark color, I think of Schopenhauer's fragile boat awash in a Dionysian storm. Rothko sits in an Apollonian calm, but it is only temporary. It is, as Nietzsche admitted, an illusion. For some, the illusion is enough to stave off the terror of what lies behind it. For others not. Rothko, I believe, had a profound understanding of both impulses, as well as the precarious balancing act he had to maintain between them. His art was at once the lifeboat and the storm.

4.

A jazz pianist named Sonny would have been a contemporary of Rothko's and would have lived only twenty blocks away, in Harlem, were he real and not a character in a James Baldwin short story, "Sonny's Blues." Still I think of Rothko and Sonny together. Both suffered great torment, and both took their own art to the brink of the Dionysian void. Neither could rely on language to make sense of it, or any art form that had come before. I also bring up Sonny because he knows something vital: He knows that only his art can save him. And in that, I think he can tell us something about his contemporary Mark Rothko.

"Sonny's Blues" is narrated by an unnamed high school math teacher who doesn't understand music and doesn't understand his younger brother, Sonny. The story begins with the older brother reading in the paper on his way to work that Sonny has been busted for possession of heroin. Oddly, the narrator can draw only one conclusion—that Sonny is trying to kill himself. Later that day, when he sees a friend of Sonny's, he asks him why Sonny wants to die. The friend replies, "He don't want to die. He wants to live. Don't nobody want to die, ever." And though the narrator had vowed years before to their mother that he would look after Sonny, he turns his back on his brother when Sonny is sent to prison. Not until his own daughter dies of polio does the narrator write Sonny. "My troubles made his real," he tells us. Feeling guilt that he has not been a better keeper of his brother, or that he never tried to understand Sonny's dark inwardness, the narrator picks Sonny up when he is released from prison and asks him to come live with him and his wife. Sonny begins to reconnect with musicians he knows in the Village, and his brother looks for signs that Sonny may be using again. One afternoon, the two of them watch a Harlem street singer wailing to a crowd a song called "'Tis the Old Ship Zion."

> As the singing filled the air the watching, listening faces underwent a change, the eyes focusing on something within; the music seemed to soothe a poison out of them; and time seemed, nearly to fall away from the sullen, belligerent, battered faces, as though they were fleeing back to their first condition, while dreaming of their last.

Later, over a beer, Sonny tries to explain to his brother, "Her voice reminded me for a minute of what heroin feels like sometimes— when it's in your veins. It make you feel sort of warm and cool at the same time. And distant. And—and sure. It makes you feel—in control. Sometimes you've got to have that feeling." Frightened, Sonny's brother grows contemptuous, scared, angry. He is a man who accepts with a stubborn fatalism the limitations of a black man's life in Harlem in the fifties. The idea that one might try to "control" one's destiny would simply not occur to him. But Sonny wants badly for his brother to understand the lure of heroin, because what he really wants his brother to understand is the lure—the power, the uses—of art. "Listening to that woman sing," Sonny says, "it struck me all of a sudden how much suffering she must have had to go through—to sing like that. It's *repulsive* to think you have to suffer that much." His brother replies, "But there's no way not to suffer—is there, Sonny?" Sonny smiles and says, "I believe not, but that's never stopped anyone from trying. . . . No, there's no way not to suffer. But you try all kinds of ways to keep from drowning in it, to keep on top of it, and to make it seem—well, like *you*. Like you did something, all right, and now you're suffering for it. You know? . . . why *do* people suffer? Maybe it's better to do something to give it a reason, *any* reason."

But if there's no way not to suffer, Sonny's pragmatic brother reasons: "Isn't it better, then, just to—take it?" Sonny explodes, "But nobody just takes it. That's what I'm telling you! *Everybody* tries not to. You're just hung up on the *way* some people try—it's not *your* way!"

Sonny has considered the Judeo-Christian logic that to suffer for no reason is unbearable: We must have done something wrong; we must *deserve* to suffer. That is one way—it was my grandfather's way—to make it feel "like you." But as an artist, Sonny will ultimately choose the more Nietzschean way to get control of his own suffering. Rather than trying to escape it, he will face up to the stink, the funk, the "storm inside," because to face up to it means to get control of it, to give it form, to make it you. Sonny *is* Nietzsche's tragic artist: He will stare down a life that is racially, economically, existentially *unjust*—a life that *may not be worth living*—and he will save himself with his art. Wrote Nietzsche:

> *Here, when the danger to his will is greatest, art approaches as a saving sorceress, expert at healing. She alone knows how to turn these nauseous thoughts about the horror or absurdity of existence into notions with which one can live: these are the sublime as the artistic taming of the horrible.*

Later that night, Sonny takes his brother down to a club in the Village, where he will sit in with a four-piece band. The narrator realizes that for the first time, he is in Sonny's "kingdom" and that here, Sonny is royalty. He's nobody's brother. He's Sonny. On the bandstand, Sonny sits down at the piano. A large Mingus-like character named Creole dictates the tempo from his bass fiddle. "He was having a dialogue with Sonny," his brother writes. "He wanted Sonny to leave the shoreline and strike out for the deep water. He was Sonny's witness that deep water and drowning are not the same thing." And slowly, Sonny does venture out into the Dionysian storm. And his brother realizes that "the man who creates the music is hearing something else, is dealing with the roar rising from the void and imposing order on it as it hits the air. What is evoked in him, then, is of another order, more terrible because it has no words, and triumphant, too, for that same reason." Sonny launches further, filling his instrument with "the breath of life, his own." He is rewriting, in each moment, the song "Am I Blue?" Desperately, Sonny retrieves the painful facts of his own life and grafts them onto the ephemeral string of notes as they hit the air. His brother hears "with what burning he had made it his, with what burning we had yet to make it ours, how we could cease lamenting. Freedom lurked around us and I understood, at last, he could help us to be free if we would listen." The narrator suddenly thinks of his dead parents, of his dead little girl, and he thinks of how Sonny is taking all this into himself and "was giving it back" in a way that, in his words, we can stand it, in a way that we can even find beauty in it.

The song ends. People applaud. The narrator sends a Scotch and milk up to the bandstand. Sonny sips it, looks back at his brother, then sets the drink on the piano. It glows there like the song itself, which has taken the storm and given it shape. It is "the very cup of trembling."

I think of Sonny sitting at his piano after his solo, and Rothko sitting in his deck chair after a session of painting. For a moment, both have tamed Schopenhauer's storm; they are safe, in control. They are each the Apollonian artist who refuses to yield to the storm and does not yearn to escape it. They haven't succumbed—at least not yet—to heroin, poverty, chronic depression. Sonny's brother had been unwilling to accept heroin as a way to "control" one's suffering; to him, it was a way of giving in, of giving up: it was suicide. And in the end, without saying so, Sonny agrees. Religion can't save him; nor smack. There's only his art. In this moment, Sonny and Rothko have forced Proteus to take shape, and they have wrestled him to the beach. Through jazz and abstract painting, Sonny and Rothko adopt the most demanding of mediums—entirely new vocabularies—to tell the story of suffering in a way that we can hear it new. After all, says Sonny's brother, "There isn't any other tale to tell."

5.

For my father's funeral, my grandmother insisted on an open casket over my mother's objection. Though the undertaker had done his best to repair the rifle's damage, my father's head looked bloated, unreal, freakish as he lay in state. My great-aunts and -uncles didn't even know he had committed suicide until they arrived in Virginia for the funeral and read it in the local paper. My grandmother had simply told them he had "gone to be with the Lord," as if he were a Buddhist monk leaving his family behind to wander the Wu Mountains. My grandmother, at least, understood the dire implications of Matthew 10:37: "He who loves his father and mother more than me is not worthy of me." Here was proof that her son was worthy.

And this is the thing that my mother, a forgiving woman, will not forgive—my grandmother smiled throughout the entire funeral. Even Job raged for thirty chapters at God's seeming injustice, until the voice of the whirlwind finally grew tired of his harangue and ground Job's face in the dirt. My grandmother did not need such convincing. If she ever mourned her son, she did it alone. In public, she wore the veil of stoic fortitude. If it was God's will to take her oldest son, she would show everyone that she understood, that she would accept that burden of fate, that she too loved the Lord even more than her own family.

I don't mean to suggest that my grandmother was a cruel woman. In the years following my father's death, I was closer to her than anyone besides my mother. When I stayed with my grandparents during the summers, she would read to me for hours from Howard Garis's *Uncle Wiggily* books, and I would make her tape record each session so that I could listen to them over and over when I returned home. But after my father's death, she slowly began to shut down and close off. I know, because she told me, that she never cried after my father died. She became a model of virtue for my grandfather's congregation, a distant model, rarely available to anyone who might need her help.

No tenet of the Christian theology seems so vacuous to me as the one always trotted out at times of tragedy: that things happen *for a reason*. God is rational; we simply, in our blindness, cannot understand his rationale. And because God has a plan, my grandmother could smile through her grief, assured that in the end it could, and would, all make sense. It seems too awful to consider the alternative—that things don't happen for a reason, that they just happen. Yet this is precisely what Nietzsche admired about the early Greeks: that they faced up to a world *without explanation* and out of it made their *own meaning*.

Of suffering, Baldwin's artist, Sonny, said, "No one just takes it. You try all kinds of ways to keep from drowning in it." Not my grandmother. She just took it. What seems so terrible, as I think back over the last forty years of her life, is that, unlike Sonny, she could not find a use for her suffering, she couldn't turn it into something else, and it slowly buried her in a shell of unfeeling that gradually slid into dementia.

6.

According to the Hebrew creation story, written about six thousand years ago, the first man was sculpted from *adammah*—"red clay." But to reach back at least twenty thousand more years to the caves at Lascaux and Altamira, one is struck by how the earliest painters we know conceived of their horses, bison, and aurochs with the same reds, maroons, and blacks that we see in the Rothko Room. Like the sand painters of the American Southwest, the Magdalenian artists of the Upper Paleolithic era derived their powdered colors from the iron oxides within or around the caves where they painted. The Navajo sand painter took his brown from juniper root, his black from sumac. The Magdalenian artists painted with the same ochers, deep reds, and blacks. Near the frescoes, archaeologists have found mortars and pestles the painters used to grind pigment. There is also evidence that the artists heated ocher colors to achieve the manganese tints that gave shape to the massive, reddish-black fauna that stampede along the walls. Rothko, who had spent the fifties experimenting with vast combinations of color, at the end decided to return to these powerful hues of the beginning, the hues of earth, blood, and fire. He returned to the palette of the most primitive ritual.

And whereas Rothko evoked breathing as a sacral metaphor for applying paint, scholars now think that the cave painters at Lascaux and Altamira actually *did* blow pigment onto the cave walls through the hollow bones of griffin vultures—the same bones out of which they made the first flutes and thus the first music—and did so as a spiritual act. Says French prehistorian Michel Lorblanchet, "Spitting is a way of projecting yourself onto the wall, becoming one with the horse you are painting. Thus the action melds you with the myth." The breath becomes the invisible syntax that binds all living things. The early cave painters were enacting what Nietzsche called a "unity of being," a ritual that psychology and anthropology have identified as characteristic of the primitive mind. In this early consciousness, the individual ego was weak; rather Neolithic man projected himself everywhere onto the world, and thus found kinship with the reindeer and ox. Yet the history of Western consciousness has been a withdrawal from this unity into ever-hardening distinctions. Socratism, Platonism, and Pauline Christianity were long exercises in division, splitting the good from evil, the living from the dead, the I from thou, the body from the soul, the human from the rest of the living world.

Like the Neolithic painters, Rothko's work can be read as an attempt to overcome the false boundaries of the self. He dismissed the label "abstract expressionist" on the grounds that he had nothing personal he wanted to convey. "I don't express myself in my painting," he once said, "I express my not-self." If mimetic art captured the world's ephemera, including the self, then Rothko's abstract painting expressed the sublime spirit that we associate with the transcendental. Rothko once dismissed the social realist painter Ben Shahn as a "journalist," which is to say, Shahn painted the characters, the *scene*, whereas Rothko painted the primordial chorus— he painted tragedy itself. He had taken his cue from Nietzsche that this was the more heroic, elemental task. Rothko had gone so far down into what Yeats called "the deep-heart's core" that there *are* no images to contain what the painter finds there. It cannot be given form; the language of images cannot accommodate it. It is the imageless image: the face we had before we were born. It is the place to which the suicide returns.

7.

In her poem "The Rothko Room," Gillian Clarke refers to the smoke-like threshold in each painting as a "scaffolding of pain." That is about as exact an image as one can find for these imageless, interior landscapes. To pass through those ciphers is to disappear into something final and inescapable. The exact opposite could be said about the thin black rectangles that stand about a sky-blue background in Robert Motherwell's *Open* series of paintings. As the titles suggest, those thresholds call us back into a kind of ontological clearing where religion and philosophy fall away and, in Martin Heidegger's phrase, we "let Being: be." Those paintings feel almost utopian in both their aim and execution. They are exhilarating. Motherwell's portal is pulling us into the open of Rilke's *Eighth Duino Elegy,*

> *that pure space into which flowers*
> *endlessly open. . . .*
> *that pure*
> *unseparated element which one breathes*
> *without desire and endlessly knows..*
>
> [trans. Stephen Mitchell]

Beyond Motherwell's thresholds await the pastoral, the prelapsarian, the unfallen world. These openings exist in time. But Rothko could see only a violent journey into the abyss. Motherwell shows us a way back into the world. For Rothko, there is no way back. Only a way out.

8.

At the end of "Sonny's Blues," the bassist, Creole, pushes Sonny "to leave the shoreline and strike out for the deep water." Which he does. His piano is his Schopenhauerian lifeboat, and he embarks on a brilliant solo that takes in all his psychic chaos, all Harlem's pain, and give it shape, makes it bearable. Then, in the end, Sonny's piano also leads him back to shore. Safe. For now. Sonny's blues, his brother finally realizes, was an act of enormous risk and courage.

Unlike Sonny, my father never returned to shore, never came back to his family, never made sense of his own chaos. In *The Birth of Tragedy*, Nietzsche said that only the gods or art can save us from the urge for nothingness. Art saved Sonny, but it couldn't save my father. Nor could religion, because unlike the Greek gods, who *justified life by living it,* my family's religion viewed this life as something separate from God, unjustifiable, fallen. But if *I* were to remain alive, that was a theology I had to reject. Living alone in Oxford that semester gave me the distance I needed to begin to find a path away from my family's own tragic encumbrance with religion. That path began with art: the art of the Tate Gallery and the literature I read there on the banks of the Thames. Nietzsche had convinced me that art, like the gods, could justify living. Art could give life the texture and the intensity that was its own justification.

But that wasn't enough for my father, because the work of art is, finally, an act of sublimation, a return to the shoreline. When viewers speak, as we inevitably do, of Rothko's painting as sublime, we mean that, standing before them, we are in the presence of something that transcends the human, that transcends our understanding. And yet on some almost unspeakable level, it speaks to us. About things that have not yet risen to the level of language, about images that have no image, about the self that exists before and beyond the self. But we can never remain on the plain of the sublime. We leave the museum. We have to return it to the level of language, as I have done here. Unless . . .

Unless one takes one's own life. Suicide is the one sublime act that can never be sublimated. The suicide will never return to find accommodation within the father's house. To raise the sword against oneself is to find release into a moment—an endless moment—of freedom. Standing before the dark thresholds of the Rothko Room, I began to understand that. I began to understand something vital about the father I had never known.

ACKNOWLEDGMENTS

Versions of these essays appeared, sometimes under different titles, in the following magazines and journals:

Orion:	"Notes from A Very Small Island," "The New Creationism"
Harper's (online):	"The Circulatory System: A Manifesto" (published as "The End of Illth")
The Sun:	"In the Land of Rock and Sky"
Dissent:	"Instead of the Ten Commandments"
Garden & Gun:	"Birding With Wendell Berry"
Southern Humanities Review:	"Lionspeak"
Terrain and the anthology *The Edge of the Fourth Genre:*	"Speak and Bear Witness"
Subtropics:	"Remembering Guy Davenport"
Ecotone:	"A Week on the Kentucky River ..."
Artkrush:	"Nine Drafts of a Suicide Note"

I would like to express my appreciation to all of the editors who worked on these pieces, but first and foremost I want to thank the relentlessly exacting Jennifer Sahn, formerly of *Orion* magazine.

My many thanks also to: Jin Auh of the Wylie Agency, Melissa Young, Wyatt Mason, Mary Chandler Bolin, Jim Krupa, Joe Wilkins and the Blue Mountain Center.

Printed in the United States
by Baker & Taylor Publisher Services